DOING TRIANGULATION AND MIXED METHODS

Doing Triangulation and Mixed Methods by Uwe Flick is the ninth volume in *The SAGE Qualitative Research Kit*. This book can be used together with the other titles in the *Kit* as a comprehensive guide to the process of doing qualitative research, but is equally valuable on its own as a practical introduction to doing triangulation and mixed methods.

Fully updated and expanded to ten volumes, this second edition of the *Kit* presents the most extensive introduction to the state-of-the-art of qualitative research.

COMPLETE LIST OF TITLES IN *THE SAGE QUALITATIVE RESEARCH KIT*

- *Designing Qualitative Research* **Uwe Flick**
- *Doing Interviews* **Svend Brinkmann and Steinar Kvale**
- *Doing Ethnography* **Amanda Coffey**
- *Doing Focus Groups* **Rosaline Barbour**
- *Using Visual Data in Qualitative Research* **Marcus Banks**
- *Analyzing Qualitative Data* **Graham R. Gibbs**
- *Doing Conversation, Discourse and Document Analysis* **Tim Rapley**
- *Doing Grounded Theory* **Uwe Flick**
- *Doing Triangulation and Mixed Methods* **Uwe Flick**
- *Managing Quality in Qualitative Research* **Uwe Flick**

MEMBERS OF THE EDITORIAL ADVISORY BOARD

DOING
TRIANGULATION
AND MIXED
METHODS

UWE FLICK

THE SAGE QUALITATIVE RESEARCH KIT 2ND EDITION

Edited by Uwe Flick

Los Angeles | London | New Delhi
Singapore | Washington DC | Melbourne

SAGE Publications Ltd
1 Oliver's Yard
55 City Road
London EC1Y 1SP

SAGE Publications Inc.
2455 Teller Road
Thousand Oaks, California 91320

SAGE Publications India Pvt Ltd
B 1/I 1 Mohan Cooperative Industrial Area
Mathura Road
New Delhi 110 044

SAGE Publications Asia-Pacific Pte Ltd
3 Church Street
#10-04 Samsung Hub
Singapore 049483

Editor: Mila Steele
Editorial assistant: John Nightingale
Production editor: Victoria Nicholas
Copyeditor: Andy Baxter
Proofreader: Thea Watson
Marketing manager: Emma Turner
Cover design: Shaun Mercier
Typeset by C&M Digitals (P) Ltd, Chennai, India
Printed in the UK

Library of Congress Control Number: 2017943867

British Library Cataloguing in Publication data

A catalogue record for this book is available from the
British Library

ISBN 978-1-4739-1211-3 (pbk)

At SAGE we take sustainability seriously. Most of our products are printed in the UK using FSC papers and boards.
When we print overseas we ensure sustainable papers are used as measured by the PREPS grading system.
We undertake an annual audit to monitor our sustainability.

CONTENTS

LIST OF ILLUSTRATIONS

BOXES

FIGURES

TABLES

EDITORIAL INTRODUCTION
UWE FLICK

INTRODUCTION TO *THE SAGE QUALITATIVE RESEARCH KIT*

In recent years, qualitative research has enjoyed a period of unprecedented growth and diversification as it has become an established and respected research approach across a variety of disciplines and contexts. An increasing number of students, teachers and practitioners are facing questions and problems of how to do qualitative research – in general and for their specific individual purposes. To answer these questions, and to address such practical problems on a how-to-do level, is the main purpose of *The SAGE Qualitative Research Kit*.

The books in *The SAGE Qualitative Research Kit* collectively address the core issues that arise when we actually do qualitative research. Each book focuses on key methods (e.g. interviews or focus groups) or materials (e.g. visual data or discourse) that are used for studying the social world in qualitative terms. Moreover, the books in the *Kit* have been written with the needs of many different types of reader in mind. As such, the *Kit* and the individual books will be of use to a wide variety of users:

- *Practitioners* of qualitative research in the social sciences; medical research; marketing research; evaluation; organizational, business and management studies; cognitive science; etc., who face the problem of planning and conducting a specific study using qualitative methods.
- *University teachers* and lecturers in these fields using qualitative methods can use this series as a basis of their teaching.

- *Undergraduate and graduate students* of social sciences, nursing, education, psychology and other fields where qualitative methods are a (main) part of the university training including practical applications (e.g. when writing a thesis).

Each book in *The SAGE Qualitative Research Kit* has been written by distinguished authors with extensive experience in their field and in practice with the methods they write about. When reading the whole series of books from the beginning to the end, you will repeatedly come across some issues which are central to any sort of qualitative research – such as ethics, designing research or assessing quality. However, in each book such issues are addressed from the specific methodological angle of the authors and the approach they describe. Thus you may find different approaches to issues of quality or different suggestions for how to analyze qualitative data in different books, which will combine to present a comprehensive picture of the field as a whole.

WHAT IS QUALITATIVE RESEARCH?

It has become more and more difficult to find a common definition of qualitative research which is accepted by the majority of qualitative research approaches and researchers. Qualitative research is no longer just simply '*not* quantitative research', but has developed an identity (or maybe multiple identities) of its own.

Despite the multiplicity of approaches to qualitative research, some common features of qualitative research can be identified. Qualitative research is intended to approach the world 'out there' (not in specialized research settings such as laboratories) and to understand, describe and sometimes explain social phenomena 'from the inside' in a number of different ways:

- By analyzing experiences of individuals or groups. Experiences can be related to biographical life histories or to (everyday or professional) practices; they may be addressed by analyzing everyday knowledge, accounts and stories.
- By analyzing interactions and communications in the making. This can be based on observing or recording practices of interacting and communicating and analyzing this material.
- By analyzing documents (texts, images, film or music) or similar traces of experiences or interactions.

Common to such approaches is that they seek to unpick how people construct the world around them, what they are doing or what is happening to them in terms that are meaningful and that offer rich insight. Interactions and documents are seen as ways of constituting social processes and artefacts collaboratively (or conflictingly). All of these approaches represent ways of meaning, which can be reconstructed and analyzed with different qualitative methods that allow the researcher to develop (more or less generalizable) models, typologies, theories as ways of describing and explaining social (or psychological) issues.

HOW DO WE CONDUCT QUALITATIVE RESEARCH?

Can we identify common ways of doing qualitative research if we take into account that there are different theoretical, epistemological and methodological approaches to qualitative research and that the issues that are studied are very diverse as well? We can at least identify some common features of how qualitative research is done.

- Qualitative researchers are interested in accessing experiences, interactions and documents in their natural context and in a way that gives room to the particularities of them and the materials in which they are studied.
- Qualitative research refrains from setting up a well-defined concept of what is studied and from formulating hypotheses in the beginning in order to test them. Rather, concepts (or hypotheses, if they are used) are developed and refined in the process of research.
- Qualitative research starts from the idea that methods and theories should be appropriate to what is studied. If the existing methods do not fit with a concrete issue or field, they are adapted or new methods or approaches are developed.
- Researchers themselves are an important part of the research process, either in terms of their own personal presence as researchers, or in terms of their experiences in the field and with the reflexivity they bring to the role – as are members of the field under study.
- Qualitative research takes context and cases seriously for understanding an issue under study. A lot of qualitative research is based on case studies or a series of case studies, and often the case (its history and complexity) is an important context for understanding what is studied.
- A major part of qualitative research is based on texts and writing – from field notes and transcripts to descriptions and interpretations and finally to the presentation of the findings and of the research as a whole. Therefore, issues of transforming complex social situations (or other materials such as images) into texts – issues of transcribing and writing in general – are major concerns of qualitative research.

- If methods are supposed to be adequate to what is under study, approaches to defining and assessing the quality of qualitative research (still) have to be discussed in specific ways that are appropriate for qualitative research and even for specific approaches in qualitative research.

SCOPE OF *THE SAGE QUALITATIVE RESEARCH KIT*

Designing Qualitative Research (Uwe Flick) gives a brief introduction to qualitative research from the point of view of how to plan and design a concrete study using qualitative research in one way or another. It is intended to outline a framework for the other books in *The SAGE Qualitative Research Kit* by focusing on how-to-do problems and on how to solve such problems in the research process. The book addresses issues of constructing a research design in qualitative research; it outlines stumbling blocks in making a research project work and discusses practical problems such as resources in qualitative research but also more methodological issues like the quality of qualitative research and also ethics. This framework is filled out in more detail in the other books in the *Kit*.

Three books are devoted to collecting or producing data in qualitative research. They take up the issues briefly outlined in the first book and approach them in a much more detailed and focused way for the specific method. First, *Doing Interviews* (Svend Brinkmann and Steinar Kvale) addresses the theoretical, epistemological, ethical and practical issues of interviewing people about specific issues or their life history. *Doing Ethnography* (Amanda Coffey) focuses on the second major approach to collecting and producing qualitative data. Here again practical issues (like selecting sites, methods of collecting data in ethnography, special problems of analyzing them) are discussed in the context of more general issues (ethics, representations, quality and adequacy of ethnography as an approach). In *Doing Focus Groups* (Rosaline Barbour) the third of the most important qualitative methods of producing data is presented. Here again we find a strong focus on how-to-do issues of sampling, designing and analyzing the data and on how to produce them in focus groups.

Three further volumes are devoted to analyzing specific types of qualitative data. *Using Visual Data in Qualitative Research* (Marcus Banks) extends the focus to the third type of qualitative data (beyond verbal data coming from interviews and focus groups and observational data). The use of visual data has not only become a major trend in social research in general, but confronts researchers with new practical problems in using them and analyzing them and produces new ethical issues. In *Analyzing Qualitative Data* (Graham R. Gibbs), several practical approaches and issues of making sense of any sort of qualitative data are addressed. Special attention is paid to practices of coding, of comparing and of using computer-assisted qualitative data analysis. Here, the focus is on verbal data, like interviews, focus groups or biographies. *Doing Conversation, Discourse and Document Analysis* (Tim Rapley) extends this focus to different types of data, relevant for analyzing discourses. Here, the focus is on existing material (like documents) and on recording everyday conversations and on finding traces of discourses. Practical issues such as generating an archive, transcribing video materials and how to analyze discourses with such types of data are discussed.

Three final volumes go beyond specific forms of data or single methods and take a broader approach. *Doing Grounded Theory* (Uwe Flick) focuses on an integrated research programme in qualitative research. *Doing Triangulation and Mixed Methods* (Uwe Flick) addresses combinations of several approaches in qualitative research or with quantitative methods. *Managing Quality in Qualitative Research* (Uwe Flick) takes up the issue of quality in qualitative research, which has been briefly addressed in specific contexts in other books in the *Kit*, in a more general way. Here, quality is looked at from the angle of using or reformulating existing criteria, or defining new criteria for qualitative research. This book examines the ongoing debates about what should count as defining 'quality' and validity in qualitative methodologies and examines the many strategies for promoting and managing quality in qualitative research.

Before I go on to outline the focus of this book and its role in the *Kit*, I would like to thank some people at SAGE who were important in making this *Kit* happen. Michael Carmichael suggested this project to me some time ago and was very helpful with his suggestions in the beginning. Patrick Brindle, Katie Metzler and Mila Steele took over and continued this support, as did Victoria Nicholas and John Nightingale in making books out of the manuscripts we provided.

ABOUT THIS BOOK

UWE FLICK

Much of current qualitative research is based on approaches using single or stand-alone methods and approaches. Interviews (see Brinkmann and Kvale, 2018) or focus groups (see Barbour, 2018) are often sufficient for doing a study and answering its research questions without using other methods. In ethnography (see Coffey, 2018) a single approach is used, which can include interviewing alongside observation and other methods. Discourse analysis (see Rapley, 2018) and visual research (see Banks, 2018) have their own focuses linked to a specific methodological approach. The general and extensive attention attracted by the idea of using mixed methods shows that the contexts are growing in which a single-method approach is no longer (seen as) sufficient. The concept and use of mixed methods is one focus of this book. However, a look at the history of qualitative research and at practice within qualitative research reveals that combinations of methods are not limited to linking qualitative with quantitative research and that other concepts may take a broader approach. Triangulation is one of these concepts and is the other focus of this book. In the first edition of the *SAGE Qualitative Research Kit*, triangulation was discussed mainly as a way of extending the quality of qualitative research. Therefore, it was one of the topics of the first edition of *Managing Quality in Qualitative Research* (Flick, 2018a). But the trends and methodological discussions mentioned above show that the attention to triangulation and mixed methods now goes beyond enhancing the quality of research and focuses on planning, designing and doing qualitative research (including data collection and analysis). For these reasons, this volume has been added to the books in the second edition of the *SAGE Qualitative Research Kit*. In this sense, the book has two functions in the context of the *Kit*: as a stand-alone book it aims at giving a comprehensive account of the problems and solutions in the field when combining methodological approaches in or with qualitative research; as an addition to the other books in the *Kit*, it rounds off the framework provided by the other books at a methodological level.

CHAPTER ONE

WHY TRIANGULATION AND MIXED METHODS IN QUALITATIVE RESEARCH?

CONTENTS

CHAPTER OBJECTIVES

After reading this chapter, you should know:

- the background of triangulation;
- why it was originally introduced in social research;
- what is triangulation and what is not;
- the background of mixed methods;
- why it was originally introduced in social research;
- what is seen as mixed methods and what is not; and
- what is necessary for a first orientation about the issues unfolded in the rest of the book.

TRIANGULATION AND MIXED METHODS IN QUALITATIVE RESEARCH

Triangulation and **mixed methods** are concepts that refer to a similar idea but make it concrete in differing ways. Both are mainly recognized for combining more than one methodological approach in a study. Mixed methods are focused on combining qualitative and quantitative methods. Triangulation is broader in the kinds of methods that are combined. It is often used as a combination of several qualitative methods. At the same time, it has a broader focus for what is combined – for example, several theoretical approaches or several kinds of data. Triangulation and mixed methods are mostly discussed in alternative and separate discourses, although both discourses can profit from each other. Both concepts can be helpful for extending qualitative **research design**s (see also Flick, 2018b) for several purposes ranging from extra knowledge to confirming research findings.

TRIANGULATION IN THE HISTORY OF QUALITATIVE RESEARCH

Triangulation is a concept that is often taken up in qualitative research when issues of quality are discussed (see also Flick, 2018a). The major link between triangulation and quality of qualitative research is that triangulation means extending the activities of the researcher in the process beyond what is 'normally' done – for example, by using more than one method. However, triangulation is not limited to promoting or assuring the quality of qualitative research, but it is also used to extend the range of insights and knowledge produced in a qualitative study. Both of these aims also apply to mixed methods research, which focuses on combining qualitative and quantitative research and thus extending the research approach and making it more valuable.

The different ways of extending research activities with the aim of extending knowledge will be unfolded in this and the following chapters in some detail. To do this, we will address the theoretical and conceptual basis of triangulation in this chapter before the use of different forms of triangulation is discussed in the following chapters. Different aims, and sometimes myths and reservations are linked to triangulation. Sometimes it is discussed when qualitative research is combined with quantitative approaches in order to give its results more grounding. In general, discussion of triangulation in qualitative research began in the 1970s when Norman Denzin (1970) presented a more systematic conceptualization of triangulation. If we go back a little further in the history of qualitative research, we will find that many of the studies seen as classic studies in qualitative research have not used the concept explicitly but were run according to the principles and practices of what is now discussed as triangulation. We may also find that such practices of triangulation can be seen as a feature of qualitative (also including the use of quantitative) research, as some examples may show.

If we go back to early examples of studying social problems in the history of social research, we find works such as the 'Polish Peasant' or the 'Marienthal' study (see below). Here, we see the combination of several methodological approaches as a starting point for unfolding problems such as unemployment or migration. Combining perspectives on a social problem, William F. Whyte's (1955) classic ethnographic study of a street gang in a major city in the eastern USA in the 1940s offers, on the basis of individual observations, personal notes and other sources, a comprehensive picture of a dynamic local culture. Through the mediation of a key figure Whyte had gained access to a group of young second-generation Italian migrants. As a result of a two-year period of participant observation he was able to obtain information about the motives, values and life-awareness and also about the social organization, friendship-relations and loyalties of this local culture.

The study by Marie Jahoda, Paul Lazarsfeld and Hans Zeisel (1933/1971), *Marienthal: The Sociology of an Unemployed Community*, is one of the classic studies in qualitative research (see also Fleck, 2004). Here, psychological coping with unemployment in a village was studied in the late 1920s after the main employer of its inhabitants went bankrupt. The result is the elaboration of the leitmotif of a 'tired society' as a condensed characterization of the attitude towards life and the day-to-day practices in the village and of different types of practices in reaction to the unemployment (for example, the 'unbroken', the 'resigned', the 'desperate' and the 'apathetic'). Jahoda (1995, p. 121) has summarized the methodological procedures leading to these insights in combining approaches, such as qualitative and quantitative methods, objective facts and subjective attitudes, observations of current practices and historical material and observations with planned interviews. These principles include linking different methodological approaches (qualitative, quantitative, interviews and observation). At the same time, we find different methodological perspectives (objective facts, subjective attitudes, current and historical issues). In describing the study (1933/1971), the authors list the data they used: cadastre sheets for about 500 families, life histories, sheets for documenting the use of time, protocols, school essays, different statistical data, and historical information about the village and its institutions. Accordingly, Lazarsfeld (1960, p. 14) has made the link between qualitative and quantitative data and strategies a principle, at least for this study. According to Lazarsfeld (1960, p. 15), 'three pairs of data' were used for the analysis: 'natural sources' (statistics of library use) and data that were collected for research purposes (sheets of time use); 'objective indicators' (e.g. health statistics) and subjective statements (interviews); and 'statistics and empathic descriptions of single cases'.

Another early example of triangulation of verbal and visual data is the study by Gregory Bateson and Margaret Mead (1942). A remarkable feature of the study is the empirical approach of producing and analyzing more than 25,000 photographs, masses of filmed material, paintings and sculptures on the one hand and using ethnographic conversations about this material on the other hand. Also, in *The Polish Peasant in Europe and America* by Thomas and Znaniecki (1918–20), different sorts of data were combined: 'undesigned records' as well as an exemplary life history produced by a participant for the study. Finally, Morse (2003, p. 190) sees the work of Goffman (e.g. 1989) as an example of applying triangulation without using the term. These examples show that the use of different sorts of data was characteristic of many classic studies at the beginning of qualitative research.

Barney Glaser and Anselm Strauss and their approach of discovering grounded theories were at the core of the renaissance of qualitative research in the 1960s in the USA and in the 1970s in Europe. Not only the methodological works, but also the studies (e.g. Strauss et al., 1964), are influential and instructive. Again we find different hints for the use of what was later named triangulation. Glaser and Strauss suggest the use of different types of data, what they call 'slices of data' collected in 'a multi-faceted investigation' (1967, p. 65). They also suggest using many different sorts of data, whereas Strauss et al. (1964, p. 36) advocate employing different observers in order to increase the **reliability** of observations that were made independently of each other and comparing them.

These examples may show that the triangulation of data sources, of methods and of researchers has a long tradition in various areas of qualitative research, even if the term was not (yet or always) used. These examples also demonstrate that, in the tradition of these studies, triangulation as an empirical approach to fields and issues was employed as an instrument assessing empirical results as well as a way to gain more insights and knowledge in the research.

TRIANGULATION IN THE DISCUSSION ABOUT MIXED METHODS

When the recent discussions about mixed methods started, the existing approach of triangulation was reduced to a specific understanding. Here, the confirmation of results from one approach by those of another approach is regularly seen as its major task (see e.g. Bryman, 2004). Greene et al. (1989) have introduced this limited view in the discussion by referring to two major sources. On the one hand the concept of 'multiplism' as outlined by Cook (1985) is suggested for when it is unclear which is the best of several methodologies for a study, to triangulate the most useful or promising ones. On the other hand, referring to Mark and Shotland's (1987) suggestions of purposes for multi-method designs: (a) triangulation, which seeks convergence of findings; (b) bracketing, which seeks a range of estimates on the correct answer (or triangulation with a confidence interval); and (c) complementarity (Greene et al., 1989, p. 257). With the background of these sources, the field that covers triangulation and mixed methods as ways of engaging multiple (methods) approaches is charted as follows: triangulation is limited to obtaining 'convergence, corroboration, correspondence of results' and juxtaposed against complementarity (aiming at elaboration or enhancement), development (aiming at further **sampling**) and expansion (aiming at more breadth and range) by using multiple methods (see Greene et al., 1989, p. 259 for details).

In the following chapters of this book, we will discuss: first whether charting the field of multiple approaches in this way will underestimate the potential of triangulation in several ways; second, how far it leads to some of the current shortcomings in the discussion about mixed methods (see Flick, 2018c); third, whether it gives up the option of using triangulation as a concept to overcome some of the challenges mixed methods research is currently facing; and fourth, whether it might reduce the potential of using multiple methods within the context of qualitative research. For this purpose, I will start with a short outline of both concepts – triangulation and mixed methods – in this chapter, which then will be unfolded in more detail in the following chapters.

WHAT IS TRIANGULATION AND WHAT IS NOT?

Why triangulate?

Triangulation attracted interest as a methodological strategy for a long time in social research, in **evaluation**, and qualitative research in particular, as an obligation to use combinations of methods, of data, and of researchers for improving the **validity** of a study and to 'withstand critique by colleagues' (Mathison, 1988, p. 13). This attraction was linked for some time to the combination of convergence of results, their validation and legitimation of research by applying triangulation. However, triangulation very soon became the object of a more or less fundamental critique. Put simply, the concept of triangulation means that an issue of research is considered – or in a constructivist formulation is constituted – from (at least) two points. Normally, the consideration from two or more points is materialized by using different methodological approaches (see Chapter 2). The concept of triangulation was imported from land surveying and geodesy, where it is used as an economic method of localizing and fixing positions on the surface of the earth (see Blaikie, 1991, p. 118). The definition used in this context sees triangulation as a method of locating a point from two others a known distance apart (Clark, 1951, p. 145).

In a more metaphorical sense, Campbell and Fiske (1959) and Webb et al. (1966) introduced triangulation into general methodological discussion in the social sciences. At that point, the idea was already that the issue under study is also constituted by the methods used to study it. At that time, a rather negative reading was dominant: that the issue is possibly biased by the methods that are used and that results have to be seen as artifacts. The leading question was whether 'a **hypothesis** can survive the confrontation with a series of complementary methods of testing' (Campbell and Fiske, 1959, p. 82). This led to considerations of how to prevent such a **bias**, and 'unobtrusive' and 'nonreactive measurement' (Webb et al., 1966) were stipulated. One strategy was the combination of different measurements and methods – in a 'multitrait–multimethod matrix' (Campbell and Fiske, 1959). In this context, the metaphor of triangulation is imported 'from navigation and military strategy that use multiple reference points to locate an object's exact position' (Smith, 1975, p. 273) to the social sciences.

For a better understanding of the concept of triangulation, it might be helpful to see what is *not* meant by it. In combining methods, it does not mean that one method is used for collecting data (e.g. an interview) and another one (e.g. coding) is used for analyzing those data. This is obvious and does not need an extra term. Neither does it mean the exploratory use of qualitative methods before the actual study using a standardized method, if the exploratory study is not seen as a genuine and stand-alone part of the project, but is only used for developing a questionnaire and the results of the first step do not become part of the final results of the whole study.

WHAT IS MIXED METHODS AND WHAT IS NOT?

Why mixed methods?

The reasons given for this kind of combination – in distinction from triangulation – have a broader range. A major intention in developing this approach was to end a rigorous confrontation between qualitative and quantitative research (paradigms) and to promote a more integrative concept for research combining both fields without too much fundamental and epistemological reflection (Greene, 2007). In this sense, Bryman (1992) identifies several ways of integrating quantitative and qualitative research. Triangulation for him means to check, for example, qualitative against quantitative results. Qualitative research and quantitative research can mutually support each other and provide a fuller picture of the issue under study. They focus on structural (quantitative) or process (qualitative) aspects or link micro and macro levels (see Bryman, 1992, pp. 59–61). All in all, this classification represents a broad range of variants, some of which are determined by the idea that qualitative research captures other aspects than quantitative research and that a combination is based on their distinctiveness. Theoretical considerations are not very prominent in these variants, as the focus is more on research pragmatics.

In more recent publications, (e.g. Hesse-Biber, 2010b) this mixed approach has also been adopted from inside qualitative research (see also Chapter 5).

Creswell (2015, p. 2) has defined what mixed methods is and includes as a core assumption the combination of quantitative data (statistical trends) and qualititative data (stories and personal experiences) to draw interpretations from both for a better understanding of the issue than with one form of data. He also clarifies what he does not see as mixed methods, such as collecting two sorts of qualitative data or adding qualitative data to a quantitative design as it 'involves the collection, analysis, and integration of *both* quantitative and qualitative data' (2015, pp. 2–3).

Triangulation and mixed methods

Triangulation becomes particularly important in two ways in the context of mixed methods discussions – as an instrument assessing empirical results as well as a way to more insights and knowledge in the research – when training in empirical methods increasingly includes qualitative and quantitative research, and keywords like 'mixed methods' (Tashakkori and Teddlie, 2003a) develop a special appeal. Here again, we should examine critically whether they can really meet the expectations of a pragmatic and at the same time theoretically founded combination of research approaches – in producing knowledge and in assessing the quality of research and results. In this context, the question of how far the concept of triangulation has a special importance in the combination of reflection and pragmatism in mixing methods becomes relevant.

In the following chapters, triangulation as a methodological strategy will be inspected and further spelled out against the background of the research traditions and in the context of the current discussions. Therefore, it should not only become clear what triangulation is and how it can be applied, but also what it is not and what problems can arise from using it in qualitative research. In the second part of this book we will have a similar look at mixed methods as the more recent, complementary and sometimes concurrent concept for combining methodological approaches. Here the focus is on what it can contribute to advance qualitative research.

These brief outlines of the two central concepts discussed in this book are mainly meant to give an orientation. Both will be spelled out in more detail in the following chapters – in their features, their use, distinction and complementarity, first triangulation (Chapters 2–4) and then mixed methods (Chapters 5–6) before, in the final chapters, common issues for both will be discussed (Chapters 7–9).

● KEY POINTS

- Triangulation has a history in qualitative research that started in the context of quality promotion but has developed further towards producing more and better insights.
- To achieve better insights, it seems necessary to spell out the concept of triangulation in more detail.
- The discussion of the concept has led to more differentiation and to a switch from using triangulation as a strategy of validation to one for more reflection and more knowledge.
- It will be even better if we apply this combination of research perspectives more explicitly as a basis for selecting methods to combine in order to promote quality in qualitative research.
- Mixed methods as an approach has been developed to overcome the confrontation between qualitative and quantitative research(ers).
- Mixed methods is therefore limited to combinations of qualitative and quantitative methods.

FURTHER READING

Triangulation

Triangulation and its theoretical basis are spelled out in more detail in the following sources:

Denzin, N.K. (1989) *The Research Act*, 3rd ed. Englewood Cliffs, NJ: Prentice- Hall.

Flick, U. (1992) 'Triangulation revisited: strategy of or alternative to validation of qualitative data?', *Journal for the Theory of Social Behavior*, 22: 175–97.

Flick, U. (2018) 'Triangulation', in N.K. Denzin and Y.S. Lincoln (eds), *The SAGE Handbook of Qualitative Research*, 5th ed. London and Thousand Oaks, CA: Sage, pp. 444–61.

Mixed methods

Mixed methods and their theoretical basis are explained in more detail in the following sources:

Creswell, J.W. (2015) *A Concise Introduction to Mixed Methods Research*. Los Angeles, CA: Sage.

Greene, J.C. (2007) *Mixed Methods in Social Inquiry*. San Francisco, CA: Jossey-Bass.

CHAPTER TWO

WHAT IS TRIANGULATION?

CONTENTS

CHAPTER OBJECTIVES

After reading this chapter, you should know:

- the background and the different versions of triangulation and see their relevance for advancing qualitative research;
- the different lines of discussion referring to this concept and its use in qualitative research;
- more recent understandings of triangulation; and
- that triangulation has been a feature of many good examples of qualitative research – at least implicitly.

TRIANGULATION 1.0: DENZIN'S CONCEPT OF MULTIPLE TRIANGULATION

Aims of triangulation

In discussions in qualitative research, Denzin's conceptualization of triangulation has attracted most attention (1970, 1989). Originally, Denzin conceived triangulation generally as 'the combination of methodologies in the study of the same phenomena' (1970, p. 297). The aims of triangulation were for Denzin 'a plan of action that will raise sociologists above the personalistic biases that stem from single methodologies ... triangulation of method, investigator, theory, and data remains the soundest strategy of theory construction' (1970, p. 300).

Data triangulation

Denzin distinguished several forms of triangulation. '**Data triangulation**' refers to the use of different sources of data as distinct from using different methods in the production of data (1970, p. 301). Triangulation of data allows the researcher to reach a maximum of theoretical profit from using the same methods. Denzin differentiates data triangulation in different ways: he suggests studying the same phenomenon at different times, in various locations and with different persons. Denzin thinks that this strategy is comparable with the **theoretical sampling** of Glaser and Strauss (1967). In both cases, a purposive and systematic selection and integration of persons, populations, and temporal and local settings is employed.

Beyond that, Denzin distinguished three levels at which we can analyze persons in empirical research. (1) In surveys, individuals are often randomly sampled and linked statistically to other cases without reference to a specific context. (2) Interactions in groups, families or teams are the second level. Here, the interaction and not the (single) person is the point of reference. (3) Persons are studied as parts of collectivities – for example, members of organizations, social groups or communities. Here persons and interactions are only regarded as units in so far as they represent pressures or demands coming from the collectivity (1970, p. 302).

Investigator triangulation

As a second form, Denzin suggested '**investigator triangulation**'. This means that different observers or interviewers are employed to reveal and minimize biases coming from the individual researcher. The examples in the work of Strauss et al. (e.g. 1964, p. 36) may illustrate this strategy. However, this does not mean simply sharing the work or delegating routine practices to auxiliary workers, but the systematic comparison of different researchers' influences on the issue under study and on the results of studying it: 'When multiple observers are used, the most skilled observers should be placed closest to the data' (Denzin, 1970, p. 303).

Theory triangulation

The third type in Denzin's classification refers to using several theoretical perspectives in collecting and analyzing data and to assessing which of these perspectives is (more) useful for the analysis of a phenomenon. Again, the scope of knowledge is to be extended and put on more solid ground. Especially in fields characterized by a low degree of theoretical coherence, the use of theoretical triangulation is suggested. Denzin refers to situations in which different theories are available to explain a phenomenon. Then you can try to confirm one or another theory with the data (facts speaking for themselves: Westie, 1957) or choose the theory that seems to be most plausible or develop your own theory from the data (Denzin, 1970, p. 302). **Theory triangulation** becomes relevant when it is applied to a concrete set of data – for example, an interview protocol. An example of such a theory-comparative approach to data from different perspectives is to analyze an interview with different methods of text interpretation, which takes the theoretical background assumptions of each method into account, of each method or the researcher using them. That very varied interpretations result from such an approach is not so surprising if we take the concept of Denzin seriously. He comes to the conclusion from a (hypothetical) example: 'each perspective directs analysis to different data areas, suggests different research methods and contradicts the explanations of the other' (1970, p. 306).

The advantages of theory triangulation are, according to Denzin, that it prevents researchers from sticking to their preliminary assumptions and from ignoring alternative explanations. For this, it is necessary to make all the assumptions and have all the theories to hand at the beginning of a study (1970, p. 306). In addition to that, sociologists using theory triangulation go beyond theory-specific studies toward generalized theoretical studies (1970, p. 306). And finally, theory triangulation promotes progress in theory and research by a comparative assessment and maybe **falsification** of rival theoretical models through a purposive analysis of 'negative evidence' or through developing theoretical syntheses (p. 307).

Triangulation of methods

The strongest attention is paid to the fourth form suggested by Denzin – methodological triangulation. Here, Denzin distinguishes two alternatives: **within-method** and **between-methods triangulation**. As an example of the first, he mentions different subscales in a questionnaire for addressing the same issue. For the second, he pursues the discussion about the combination of different methods in order to limit their reactivity (according to Webb et al., 1966), when he requires overcoming the limitations of the single methods by combining them. Denzin formulated a series of principles of methodological triangulation referring to the strengths and weaknesses of the single methods and to their theoretical relevance in studying an issue or field.

In these principles, Denzin suggests not so much a naïve–pragmatic combination of methods but rather a very methods-critical process of selecting methods and a continuous assessment of methodological decisions and of their appropriateness (see Flick, 2014a, for this). The point of reference is the (concrete) issue of research and the theoretical relevance of the research questions and of the results of a study. Nevertheless, at that time, the focus of methodological triangulation was for Denzin above all to validate field research, based on 'playing each method off against the other' and assessing in the concrete context (researcher, setting, theoretical perspective) which approach is the (more) appropriate one.

Finally, Denzin outlined some problems of planning studies with multiple triangulation, such as identifying empirical issues to which the different theories can be referred. Other problems are related to resources (limited money or time) and the limited accessibility of data or sites with several approaches (see 1970, pp. 311–12). The problems mentioned here refer mainly to the accessibility of fields of research in which triangulation can be applied with the necessary consistency, and to the danger that triangulation might over-challenge the – however limited – resources of a study (see Flick, 2018b; and Chapter 8 below).

Denzin has made a comprehensive proposal for designing and applying triangulation. His original concept in the 1970s moved back and forth between the claims of validating results (by playing off methods against each other), the increase in the reliability of procedures (several methods are more reliable than one method) and the grounding of theory development through the different forms of triangulation. At some points, the constitution of issues by methods becomes neglected. Denzin repeatedly talks of applying methods to the 'same phenomenon'. In response to some of the discussions and critiques that will be presented next, and due to changing his methodological position in general, Denzin has modified some aspects of his concept of triangulation in later editions of his book *The Research Act* (e.g. 1989; see below).

LINES OF DISCUSSION

Denzin's approach to triangulation is not only the most often quoted and discussed. In addition, most of the critiques of triangulation refer directly to it. A first starting point is the concept of issues underlying the combination of different methods. Starting from an ethnomethodological position, Silverman (1985, p. 21) formulates a caveat against the idea of a 'master reality' as a point of reference for judging the adequacy of methods. He is also sceptical that several methods will lead to a total picture of a phenomenon, as each will draw a picture that has to be understood within its own logic. Mainly, he makes the criticism that – despite his actually interactionist position – Denzin assumes that different methods represent the 'same phenomenon' and that we only have to put together the resulting parts of the picture. If we follow the critique of Silverman, Denzin ignores the point that was at the beginning of the whole discussion of triangulation – for example, in the case of Webb et al. (1966), the reactivity of methods, or in different terms, that every method constitutes the issues to be studied with it in a specific way. The consequence is that a combination of surveys and field research (Fielding and Fielding, 1986), participant observation and interviews (Hammersley and Atkinson, 1983) or more generally qualitative and quantitative research will not necessarily lead to the 'same' results and that discrepancies in results falsify one or another finding. On the contrary, such a discrepancy results from the relation of method and issue in the single method, which makes it necessary to develop **criteria** for assessing congruencies and discrepancies in the results. Only then can the critique by Fielding and Fielding be ignored that multiple triangulation in the sense of Denzin is an extreme form of eclecticism (1986, p. 33).

The phenomenon under study will be marked by the researcher's theoretical conceptualization in the way it can be perceived. This conceptualization influences how methods are designed and used, and the interpretation of data (observations, answers, etc.) and results. Denzin takes this into account in his idea of theoretical triangulation. He neglects this in the (only methodological) use of triangulation as a strategy of validation by playing methods off against each other. Triangulation as a 'quasi-correlation' is in danger of ignoring or neglecting the implications of a theoretical position and of the use of methods resulting from this. The reason for this is that triangulation was (mis-)understood as a form of validation at the beginning. Thus, Fielding and Fielding (1986, p. 33) condense their critique of Denzin's conception of theoretical and methodological triangulation as that triangulation may add range and depth to an analysis, but not accuracy or 'objective' truth. Here, triangulation still has the function of contributing to further grounding of data and interpretation. This aim is pursued via more adequacy and comprehensiveness in grasping the issue under study and not by a unilateral or mutual validation of the single-method results.

In the next step we will address the question: which form of congruence of results can be achieved with triangulation? If methods that are used have different qualities, it is not so much identical results that we should expect. Rather it is complementary or convergent results that can be expected (see Flick, 2004; Kelle and Erzberger, 2004). Convergence means that results fit into each other, complement each other, lie on one level, but do not have to be congruent. This means giving up the claim that triangulation – as an equivalent to correlation – allows validating methods in results in a traditional sense. If you want to assess the complementarity of results, much more – theoretical – effort is necessary than if you want to assess congruence via correlation numerically.

In the context of qualitative research, we cannot expect such unambiguous results and criteria when judging the reliability of single methods and results. Instead, we should expect an extension of knowledge potential and an extended rather than a reduced need for (theory-driven) interpretation, as Köckeis-Stangl (1982, p. 363) makes clear.

All in all, the critique of Denzin's early concept of triangulation has focused on the idea of validating by playing off methods against each other. In particular, his assumption that different methods simply represent an object, which will be the same for every method used to study it, was criticized. Sometimes this is still the argument when triangulation in general is discussed in mixed methods research (see Bryman, 1992; or Tashakkori and Teddlie, 2003b). While updating his approach to triangulation and revising his methodological stance in general in a very comprehensive way (see Lincoln, 2004; Denzin, 2004, 2012), Denzin has accepted some of the critical points.

TRIANGULATION 2.0: SOPHISTICATED RIGOUR AS DENZIN'S REACTION TO HIS CRITICS

In later publications (e.g. Denzin, 1989, p. 246; Denzin and Lincoln, 1994, p. 2), Denzin sees triangulation in a more differentiated way. At the core of his updated version is the concept of 'sophisticated rigour': 'Interpretive sociologists who employ the triangulated method are committed to sophisticated rigor, which means that they are committed to making their empirical, interpretive schemes as public as possible' (1989, pp. 235–6).

Denzin still recognizes the claim for triangulation of overcoming the methodological limitations of single methods (1989, p. 236). At the same time, he gives up the idea of playing off methods against each other in order to test hypotheses and reacts to Silverman's (1985) critique: 'The interactionist seeks to build interpretations, not test hypotheses' (Denzin, 1989, p. 244). In reaction to Fielding and Fielding (1986), Denzin (1989, p. 246) reformulates the aims of multiple triangulation as seeking for in-depth understanding but not validity in interpretive research by using triangulation.

All in all, in his later writings, Denzin sees triangulation as a strategy on the road to a deeper understanding of an issue under study and thus as a step more toward knowledge, and less toward validity and **objectivity** in interpretation. In this version, triangulation is also no longer conceived of as a strategy for confirming findings from one approach by findings from using another approach. Rather, triangulation aims at broader, deeper, more comprehensive understandings of what is studied – and that often includes, or heads at, discrepancies and contradictions in the findings.

The subsequent discussions about triangulation moved on to different concepts, such as crystallization introduced by Richardson (2000), who suggested replacing triangulation with the metaphors of the prism and the crystal to describe attempts to combine approaches. Saukko (2003) adopted this idea in the context of cultural studies for combining not only methodological approaches but also various forms of validities. Ellingson (2009, 2011) has developed Richardson's approach into a multi-genre crystallization, which puts more emphasis on writing and re-presenting research than in earlier discussions about triangulation. In more concrete terms, this approach is based on five principles: (1) it looks for a deepened, complex interpretation, (2) combining several differing qualitative approaches for producing knowledge, and (3) including several genres of writing, based on (4) a 'significant degree of reflexive consideration of the writer's self in the process of research design', and rejecting (5) claims of objectivity and truth (Ellingson, 2011, p. 605).

The suggestions made by Richardson, Saukko and Ellingson take a strongly reflexive stance in the debate about triangulation and its limitations. At the same time they do not really contribute to clarifying how to use it, in particular in comparison with mixed methods approaches, for example.

Although referring to the original understanding of triangulation as the combination of several qualitative approaches and despite using the term 'Triangulation 2.0', Denzin does not really make a strong position and argument for how to use and maintain the concept of triangulation in the context of mixed methods and in distinction to the discussions concerning mixed methods. Instead the term triangulation is again critically replaced by concepts such as multi-genre crystallization. Despite the criticism this implies about the concept of triangulation by its original proponents, and the attempts to push it aside in the context of mixed methods, there is still a place in the field for triangulation, which requires two aspects. First, to take into account what was the original context of inventing triangulation in the methodological field – to use several qualitative approaches (Denzin, 2012, p. 82) – and second, to take into account what has been critically discussed about the original aims (validation, confirmation of results) and how abandoning these aims has led to further developing the understanding of triangulation (see Flick, 1992, 2012, for examples).

TRIANGULATION 3.0: STRONG PROGRAMME OF TRIANGULATION

In extending the metaphorical chain and driving it one step further, the concept of 'Triangulation 3.0' will be outlined next.

Triangulation: a weak and a strong programme

The discussions mentioned above can provide a starting point for re-addressing triangulation as a relevant concept in distinction from the following understandings: (1) Lincoln and Guba (1985) suggested using triangulation as a *criterion* in qualitative research; (2) Bryman (1992) sees the use of triangulation as an *assessment strategy* as a major task, when other methods and the results obtained with them are used to critically evaluate the results obtained with the first method; and (3) 'triangulation' can be used to label a rather *pragmatic combination* of methods. These ways of using triangulation might be called a *weak programme* of triangulation and should be distinguished from a strong programme of triangulation (see Flick, 2011).

In a *strong programme of triangulation*, first of all, triangulation becomes relevant as a source of *extra knowledge* about the issue in question and not just as a way to confirm what is already known from the first approach (convergence of findings). Second, triangulation is seen as an *extension* of a research programme. This also includes the systematic selection of various methods and the combination of research perspectives (see Flick, 1992). Denzin (1970, 1989) has already suggested several levels of triangulation. In addition to methodological triangulation, which is differentiated into 'within-method' (e.g. the use of different subscales within a questionnaire) and 'between-methods' triangulation, which will allow the triangulation of data, he suggested the triangulation of several investigators and of various theories. The triangulation of various methods can be applied by combining qualitative methods (e.g. interviews and participant observation), quantitative methods (e.g. questionnaires and tests), or qualitative and quantitative methods. Within-method triangulation can be realized in methods like the **episodic interview** (see Flick, 2000a; and Chapter 3), which combines question–answer parts with invitations to recount relevant situations in a narrative – both approaches have been developed against a background of theories about different forms of knowledge.

COMPREHENSIVE TRIANGULATION

After outlining the approach of a **systematic triangulation of perspectives**, we can follow up the original suggestion by Denzin and his four alternatives of triangulation. I have developed this into a more systematic model, which includes these alternatives as elements of a chain (see Table 2.1).

TABLE 2.1 Comprehensive triangulation

- Investigator triangulation→
- Theory triangulation→
- Methodological triangulation→

  ○ within-method
  ○ between-methods

- Data triangulation→
- Systematic triangulation of perspectives

Researchers interested in using the full potential of triangulation should use different researchers (investigator triangulation), either working in collaboration or independently. Ideally they would bring in different theoretical perspectives, which will lead to one of the versions of methodological (within- or between-methods) triangulation. The result would be a triangulation of different sorts of data, which then allows a systematic triangulation of perspectives, if theoretical backgrounds and different aspects of the phenomenon under study are included in the approach. How far this whole chain can be pursued in the particular research project should depend on the issue under study, the research question, and the resources for the project (see Chapter 8). Even if realized only in part, this strategy can contribute to managing and promoting the quality of qualitative research.

SYSTEMATIC TRIANGULATION OF PERSPECTIVES

The suggestion of a 'systematic triangulation of perspectives' (Flick, 1992) goes in a similar direction. Here, different research perspectives in qualitative research are triangulated in order to complement their strengths and to show their limits. The aim is not a pragmatic combination of different methods, but to take into account their theoretical backgrounds. The starting points for this suggestion are classifications of the varieties of approaches in qualitative research, which are a basis for a theoretically founded, systematic triangulation of qualitative approaches and perspectives. This will be illustrated with a study about subjective theories of trust and their use in counselling practices, which I did some time ago. In this study, I applied an interview in order to reconstruct subjective theories of counsellors. Later I applied **communicative validation** for the contents of these theories and conversation analysis to consultations done by the same counsellors. The methodological issues of this study will be followed up in more detail in Chapter 3. Here, the theoretical and methodological background of the triangulation of different methods will be the focus.

Research perspectives in qualitative research

A starting point is that there is no longer *one* single qualitative research, but that different theoretical and methodological perspectives of research with different methodical approaches and theoretical conceptions of the phenomena under study can be identified within the field of qualitative research. Several attempts to structure this field with its variety of methods and their theoretical and methodological backgrounds have been undertaken.

Lüders and Reichertz (1986, pp. 92–4) bundle up the variety of qualitative research in research perspectives 'aiming at (1) the understanding of the subjective sense of meaning, (2) at the description of social action and social milieus and (3) at the reconstruction of in-depth-structure generating meanings and actions'. For the first perspective, the concentration on the respondent's viewpoint and experiences and the 'maxim to do justice to the respondent in all phases of the research process as far as possible' are characteristic features. These goals are mostly pursued by using interview strategies. In the second perspective, methodological principles are 'documenting and describing different life-worlds, milieus and sometimes finding out their inherent rules and symbols', which are realized, for instance, through conversation analysis. In the third perspective, subjective sense, intentions and meanings as surface phenomena are differentiated from objective in-depth structures as an own level of reality that generates actions. This differentiation is methodologically realized mostly by using hermeneutic methods (Reichertz, 2004).

Bergmann (1985) distinguishes 'reconstructive methods' (for example, interviews or participant observation) and (in a strict sense of the term) 'interpretive methods' (like conversation analysis) as fundamentally different approaches. While the first group of methods is employed to *produce* data (by questions or interventions in the field) in order to *reconstruct* events and participants' viewpoints for the purpose of research, in the second group research activities are restricted to merely *recording and analyzing* social activities in their 'natural form'. Each of these approaches discloses or obstructs different points of view on the phenomena under study.

Other authors suggest comparable taxonomies of qualitative research (see also Flick, 2014a, for this). These taxonomies can be used as a starting point for a triangulation of qualitative approaches that can be founded in research perspectives.

Triangulation of various qualitative strategies

These examples show that there are different streams of qualitative research with distinctive understandings of methods and issues and with different theoretical backgrounds. This can be used for a more appropriate approach to the issue under study. Here, triangulation becomes relevant as 'an attempt to relate different sorts of data' (Hammersley and Atkinson, 1983, p. 199).

Systematic triangulation of perspectives and the sorts of data to use

Accordingly, Fielding and Fielding (1986, p. 34) suggest combining methods that capture structural aspects of a problem under study with those that focus on the essential features of its meaning for the participants. If we transfer this idea to the differentiations of qualitative research mentioned above, we should combine methods that allow producing sorts of data:

- which allow understanding subjective meanings and a description of social practices and milieus,
- while using an interpretive approach to social practices, which should be combined with a reconstructive approach to analyze viewpoints and meanings beyond a current situation or activity.

As indicated before, these differentiations (from Fielding and Fielding to Bergmann) can be combined at a methodological level by using conversation analysis together with interviews. Then we can achieve the first aim in each differentiation with conversation analysis, the second by using interviews. Triangulating these two approaches may be seen as one example of putting the intended diversity of perspectives into concrete methodological terms. Examples of other combinations could be developed (see Table 2.2). This triangulation of research perspectives allows methodological approaches like interviews and conversation analysis or interviews and participant observation to be combined in a systematic way (see Chapters 3 and 4 for examples).

DEFINITION OF TRIANGULATION

After looking at the developments of the concept over the years, we can now summarize what is to be understood as triangulation in the context of social science and especially

TABLE 2.2 Systematic triangulation of perspectives

Authors	Perspective I	Method I, for example	Perspective II	Method II, for example
Bergmann (1985)	Interpretive approaches	Conversation analysis	Reconstructive approaches	Interviews
Lüders and Reichertz (1986)	Description of social practices and social milieus	Conversation analysis	Understanding subjective sense of meaning	Interviews
Fielding and Fielding (1986)	Structural aspects of the problem	Conversation analysis	Meaning of the problem for those involved	Interviews

of qualitative research (see Box 2.1). This understanding of triangulation will be further unfolded by using the different concepts that are employed in the discussion of social science methodology and elaborated in later chapters in its concrete implementation.

BOX 2.1   DEFINITION OF TRIANGULATION

Triangulation includes researchers taking different perspectives on an issue under study or more generally in answering research questions. These perspectives can be substantiated by using several methods and/or in several theoretical approaches. Both are or should be linked. Furthermore, it refers to combining different sorts of data against the background of the theoretical perspectives that are applied to the data. As far as possible, these perspectives should be treated and applied on an equal footing and in an equally consequent way. At the same time, triangulation (of different methods or data sorts) should allow a principal surplus of knowledge. For example, triangulation should produce knowledge at different levels, which means going beyond the knowledge made possible by one approach and thus contributing to promoting quality in research.

TRIANGULATION BETWEEN CONSTRUCTING ISSUES, PRODUCING KNOWLEDGE AND ASSURING RESULTS

From the theoretical and methodological discussions about the concept of triangulation that we have outlined here, several conclusions can be drawn for our context. The critiques of Denzin's original concept make clear that we should take into account that every method constitutes its issue in a specific way. Simple congruence in studying the 'same' object should not be expected from triangulating different methods. Rather, a triangulation of different methodological approaches can show different forms of constituting an issue, which may complement or contradict each other. Triangulation does not produce congruent or contradictory representations of an object, but shows different constructions of a phenomenon – for example, at the level of everyday knowledge and at the level of practices. Triangulation will be appropriate and elucidating when not only methods are linked, but also the theoretical perspectives attached to them. As the discussion so far has shown, a contemporary concept of triangulation will not be limited to an assessment of the validity of results only, but it will also be about the collection of more knowledge.

Finally, it is legitimate to talk of triangulation if the different approaches have the same relevance in planning a study, and in collecting and analyzing the data, and if they are applied consistently. The different concepts of triangulation outlined in this chapter provide a basis for a reflected use of this strategy in the context of quality promotion in qualitative research. Common to them is that triangulation should be more than a simple and pragmatic combination of two or more methods and that we should avoid a 'more of the same' strategy in triangulation. If we start from a systematic triangulation of perspectives, the contribution to quality promotion will be most fruitful. In the following chapters, we will transfer this discussion to a more methodological level and continue our discussion with respect to the level of research practice, when we address several alternatives for how to make methodological triangulation work.

KEY POINTS

- The discussion of the concept of triangulation has led to more differentiation and to a switch from using triangulation as a strategy of validation to one allowing more reflection and more knowledge in the process of a qualitative study.
- Comprehensive triangulation is an approach to using the methodological potential of this strategy most consistently when it comes to using triangulation in qualitative research.
- Triangulation will be methodologically sound if we take into account that we implicitly combine research perspectives when combining methods.
- It will be even sounder if we apply this combination of research perspectives more explicitly as a basis for selecting methods to combine in order to advance qualitative research.
- A strong programme of triangulation will go beyond confirming results and will combine methods as diverse as possible and as needed in the concrete research project.

FURTHER READING

Triangulation and its theoretical basis are spelled out in more detail in the following sources:

Denzin, N.K. (1989) *The Research Act*, 3rd ed. Englewood Cliffs, NJ: Prentice-Hall.

Denzin, N.K (2012) 'Triangulation 2.0', *Journal of Mixed Methods Research*, 6: 80–8.

Flick, U. (1992) 'Triangulation revisited: strategy of or alternative to validation of qualitative data?', *Journal for the Theory of Social Behavior*, 22: 175–97.

Flick, U. (2018) 'Triangulation', in N.K. Denzin and Y.S. Lincoln (eds), *The SAGE Handbook of Qualitative Research*, 5th ed. London and Thousand Oaks, CA: Sage, pp. 444–61.

CHAPTER THREE

METHODOLOGICAL TRIANGULATION IN QUALITATIVE RESEARCH

CONTENTS

CHAPTER OBJECTIVES

After reading this chapter, you should understand:

- the principles of combining different approaches in one method;
- the links between theory triangulation and methodological triangulation; and
- the relevance of both for qualitative research.

When triangulation is discussed in the context of qualitative research, most authors refer to methodological triangulation. The basic idea here is that using more than one method will open up several perspectives for understanding issues in qualitative research compared to a single-method study. Here again, we find several suggestions for how to combine different methods and which sorts of methods should be combined. Denzin had already distinguished in his concept of triangulation between 'within-method' and 'between-methods', and the latter meant the triangulation of several stand-alone methods. In what follows, the first strategy will be spelled out a little more by using several examples, before the triangulation of several (qualitative) methods is discussed. Denzin (1970) mentions the example of using different sub-scales in a questionnaire as an example of within-method triangulation.

WITHIN-METHOD TRIANGULATION: THE CASE OF THE EPISODIC INTERVIEW

If we apply this idea to qualitative research, it means combining different methodo-logical approaches in one qualitative method. These approaches include different aims and theoretical backgrounds, but do not go beyond the scope of one method (see Figure 3.1).

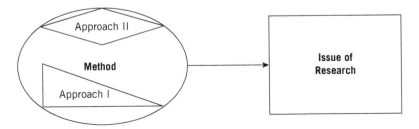

FIGURE 3.1 Within-method triangulation

Depending on how method or methodological approach is understood, we could use ethnography as an example (see Coffey, 2018; and Chapter 4 below). Here, method is to be understood as a procedure combining several methodological approaches. As an example of this form of triangulation I will discuss the episodic interview (see Flick, 2000a, 2014a). This method combines questions and narratives in approaching a specific issue – for example, everyday knowledge about technological change (see Flick, 1994, 1995), or health concepts of lay people (see Flick, 2000b) or of professionals (see Flick et al., 2003, 2004).

Triangulation of theoretical perspectives in one method

This method was developed against a specific theoretical background, which is informed by more recent discussions and findings regarding the psychology of memory and knowledge. Here we find a distinction between **narrative-episodic** and **semantic-conceptual knowledge**. The first is more oriented to situations, their context and progress, whereas the second knowledge is more abstract, generalized and decontextualized from specific situations and events and oriented to concepts, definitions and relations. The first can be accessed more easily in narratives, the second more easily with (argumentative) statements. Narratives (see Brinkmann and Kvale, 2018) are more context-sensitive for the setting in which experiences are made than other, more semantic models of knowledge. However, knowledge that abstracts more from such contexts is developed from a multitude of similar, generalizable experiences – for example, as knowledge of concepts and rules. More so than in narratives, which are centred upon the particular (Bruner, 1990, 2002), semantic knowledge represents normal, rule-based and generalized knowledge across a multitude of situations and experiences. This again is episodically concretized and fleshed out in narrative knowledge: 'Rules and maxims state significant generalisations about experience but stories illustrate and explain what those summaries mean' (Robinson and Hawpe, 1986, p. 124).

Such abstract parts of knowledge are rather grouped around conceptual meanings and their (semantic) relations. This does not mean that narrative knowledge would not aim at meanings. The term 'semantic knowledge' has been used for some time following models of semantic memory and is based on a rather limited concept of meaning compared with narrative knowledge (Bruner, 1990). Semantic models of knowledge were conceptualized following models of semantic memory, which have been studied in the cognitive psychology of memory for some time. Tulving gives as a definition:

Semantic memory is the memory necessary for the use of language. It is a mental thesaurus, organized knowledge a person possesses about words and other verbal symbols, their meaning and referents, about relations among them, and about rules, formulas, and algorithms for the manipulation of these symbols, concepts and relations. (1972, p. 386)

If we transfer this principle to the various models of semantic knowledge developed over time, we can summarize that they consist of concepts linked by semantic relations. Similar to memory, semantic-conceptual knowledge is complemented by episodic parts. The starting point is Tulving's (1972) juxtaposition of semantic and episodic memory, which, in addition to concepts, includes memories of concrete situations. It is central for a conception of episodic memory or knowledge that it is not concepts and their relations that are its basis, but memories of specific situations, events or cases from one's own experience. This means that a central feature of knowledge and memory according to this approach are concrete situations with their components: location, time, what happens, who is involved, and so on. Regarding the contents of episodic knowledge it should be stated that it consists not only of autobiographical memory but of situation-related knowledge in general (Strube, 1989). This situational knowledge in the episodic knowledge or memory is the basis for 'generalising across concrete events, which produces general knowledge from episodic knowledge by decontextualisation and this general knowledge has lost the memory of time and localization' (1989, p. 12). General experiential knowledge is based on the generalization of knowledge, which was first collected and stored in reference to situations. It has lost its situational specificity when it is transferred to other, similar situations and general concepts and rules of interrelations have developed. Both parts are complementary parts of world knowledge. This means that 'world knowledge' consists of various components: clearly episodic parts referring to specific situations with their concrete (local–temporal, etc.) features; clearly semantic parts with concepts and relations that are abstracted from such concrete situations; and gradual forms of mixing and blending like schemata of events and processes.

According to this juxtaposition of concrete-episodic and abstract-conceptual knowledge, a reflection of such models of storing knowledge and meaning-making with episodic knowledge becomes relevant as a primary form of meaning-making based on meaningful episodes (Polkinghorne, 1988, p. 1). The analysis of knowledge referring to situations and episodes becomes particularly relevant in this context.

Several approaches in one method

In interviews, the parts of everyday knowledge mentioned so far are more or less explicitly approached. On the one hand, semi-structured interviews can include narratives (Brinkmann and Kvale, 2018). Mishler (1986) has studied what happens when interviewees in semi-structured interviews start to narrate and how these narratives are treated, and has shown that they are suppressed rather than taken up. In narrative interviews (Flick, 2014a, Chapter 18), interviewees often switch during a narrative to descriptions, argumentations and other non-narrative forms of presentation. In this method, such forms of presentation are intentional in the last (balancing) part of the interview; in the narrative main part they are rather deviations from the ideal. However, an approach of within-method triangulation would suggest using both areas of knowledge systematically and a purposeful combination of approaches to both. According to such aims, the episodic interview was designed as a method to collect the components of everyday knowledge as outlined in Figure 3.2.

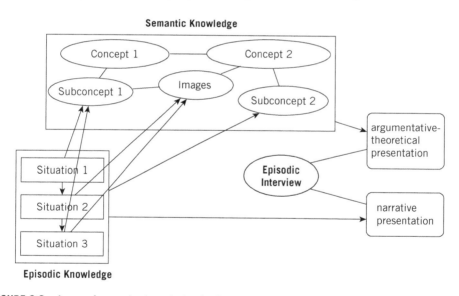

FIGURE 3.2 Areas of everyday knowledge in the episodic interview

The central element of this form of interview is that you recurrently ask the interviewee to present narratives of situations (e.g. 'If you look back, what was your first encounter with television? Could you please recount that situation for me?'). Also, you will mention chains of situations ('Please, could you recount how your day went yesterday, and where and when technology played a part in it?'). You will prepare an interview guide in order to orient the interview to the topical domains for which such a narrative is required. To familiarize the interviewee with this form of interview, its basic principle is first explained (e.g. 'In this interview, I will ask you repeatedly to recount situations in which you have had certain experiences with technology in general or with specific technologies'). A further aspect is the interviewee's imaginings of expected or feared changes ('Which developments do you expect in the area of computers in the near future? Please imagine, and tell me a situation that would make this evolution clear for me'). Such narrative incentives are complemented by questions in which you ask for the interviewee's subjective definitions ('What do you link to the word "television" today?'). Also, you will ask for abstractive relations ('In your opinion, who should be responsible for change due to technology, who is able to or should take the responsibility?'). This is the second large complex of questions aimed at accessing semantic parts of everyday knowledge.

Concepts of health and ageing as an example

The principle and structure of the episodic interview will be demonstrated using the interview schedule from our study on professionals' health concepts (see Flick et al., 2003, 2004), which includes three major components:

- Questions and narrative stimuli referring to the interviewee's health concepts.
- Questions and narrative stimuli concerning health in old age.
- Questions and narrative stimuli referring to prevention and health promotion.

In this study, general practitioners and home-care nurses were interviewed. Health concepts were addressed with questions concerning doctors' and nurses' subjective concepts of health and their relevance for professional work and with narrative stimuli referring to them. It was instructive to see what were recounted as concrete situations, but also the selection taken from a varied host of descriptions of situations that would also have been possible. This shows the events causing health concepts to be developed or changed. We assumed that health concepts and practices change in the course of a life, as both have a biographical component and are modified by specific personal (e.g. illness) or professional experiences (with patients or resulting from further education). Furthermore, we were interested in links between subjective health concepts and practices and the professional handling of the issue. A background assumption here is that the issue of health allows you, less than illness does, to keep a distance for oneself from professional work.

The second complex of questions and narrative stimuli focused on health promotion. It aimed at the professionals' understanding of this issue and at gaining information about the part prevention and health promotion played in their day-to-day practices. This could reveal the relevance of health promotion in the professional routines of doctors and nurses. It could also show how far discussion of public health, prevention and health promotion have influenced medical and nursing practices.

The third complex addressed concepts of health in old age and the professionals' attitudes towards prevention and health promotion in their work with (very) old people. We also asked for an evaluation of the professionals' own training and how much it helped in later professional confrontation with health and old age.

Box 3.1 includes excerpts from the interview guide. Here, the narrative stimuli addressing episodic knowledge are labelled as E-1, etc.; questions addressing semantic knowledge are marked as S-2, etc. Using this interview guide led to the presentation of the concept in the form of a definition (in this case of health), as in the following example:

I: What is that for you, 'health'? What do you link with the word 'health'?

IP: With the word 'health', well quite a lot, not only free of illness, but a feeling well all around, to feel well mentally as well, to feel well socially, that means in the social frame you live and so on … Yes, one could maybe say also, free of financial concerns, what is surely part of it, because financial concerns make you ill, too.

BOX 3.1   EXAMPLE OF AN INTERVIEW GUIDE FOR AN EPISODIC INTERVIEW

Concepts of health and ageing

In this interview, I will repeatedly ask you to tell me situations in which you have had experiences with the issues of 'health' and 'ageing'.

S-1   What is that for you, 'health'? What do you link with the word 'health'?

E-2   What has influenced your idea of health in particular? Can you please tell me an example that makes this clear for me?

E-3   Do you have the impression that your idea of health has changed in the course of your professional life? Please tell me a situation that makes this clear for me.

(Continued)

(Continued)

E-4 Do you have the impression that the way you handle the issue of health has changed compared to earlier times? Can you please tell me an example that makes this clear for me?

E-5 Do you have the feeling that your private practices referring to health influence your professional practice? Can you please tell me an example that makes this clear for me?

E-6 What does it mean for you, to promote health in your professional practice? Can you please tell me an example that makes this clear for me?

E-7 Have your professional practices changed in the last few years in what concerns the promotion of health? Can you please tell me an example that makes this clear for me?

E-8 Would you please tell me how your day went yesterday? How, when and where did the promotion of health play a role in it?

S-9 What does '(old) age' mean for you? What are your associations with that term?

E-10 What role does 'age' play in your life? Could you please tell me a typical situation?

E-11 When you think back, what was your most important experience with 'age' in your professional life? Could you please tell me a typical situation?

E-12 Do you have the impression that your idea of age has changed in the course of your professional life? Please tell me a situation that makes this clear for me.

E-13 What makes it clear for you, in your professional life, that a person is old? Could you please tell me an example of this?

S-14 What does 'health in older age' mean for you?

E-15 Do you have the impression that your professional training has prepared you sufficiently for the issues of 'health' and 'ageing'? Please tell me a situation that makes your impression clear for me.

S-16 If you think of health promotion and prevention in your professional work, what relevance should they have for senior citizens?

S-17 Was there anything in the interview that was missing for you or anything you found annoying?

On the other hand, the interviews provided narratives, for example about how changes were initiated:

I: What has influenced your idea of health in particular? Can you please tell me an example that makes this clear for me?

IP: There are actually very many examples. Well influenced, my personal opinion is simply influenced by the fact that our children, we have three children and the three big ones, when they were born, that was 19 and 18, 17 years ago, were both very sick. For our son, the older one, we did not know if he survived the first night. And then I had the feeling that a switch turned in me, yeah? Well was turned. Up to then, I needed always a lot of formal security, local security, financial security, and that became completely unimportant for me from that day, when the decision was so much in the air. And at that time, I have started to develop my own relation to conventional medicine. I have traditional school medicine training and I have then started to organize many things in the family in another way first, by talking, by physiotherapy, by acupuncture, ozone/oxygen therapy. And as that worked quite well, I have applied it with patients, too.

Finally, we found mixtures of definitions and narratives of how the interviewee has developed this definition and what played a role in this:

I: What is that for you, 'health'? What do you link with the word 'health'?

IP: Health is relative, I think. Someone can be healthy, too, who is old and has a handicap and can feel healthy nevertheless. Well, in earlier times, before I came to work in the community, I always said, someone is healthy if he lives in a very well ordered household, where everything is correct and super-exact, and I would like to say, absolutely clean? But I learned better, when I started to work in the community ... I was a nurse in the [name of the hospital] before that, in intensive care and arrived here with completely different ideas. And I had to learn that anyone should be accepted in his domesticity the way he is. And therefore, I think, health is – it always depends on how someone feels. Well, someone can have a disease, and feel healthy nevertheless. I think that's how it is.

Representations of technological change in everyday life as an example

For the situations that are recounted in an episodic interview, we can distinguish several types, as the following examples from our study on the **social representations** of technological change may demonstrate (see Flick, 1996). First, we found that episodes – concrete situations, a specific event – that the interviewee has experienced, were recounted or mentioned:

I: When you remember, what was your first experience with technology? Could you please tell me that situation?

IP: Well, I can remember the day when I learned cycling, my parents put me on the bicycle, one of these small children's bikes, sent me off, it was not that long, that I went by myself, my father gave me some push and let me off, and then I continued to ride until the parking lot ended and then I fell on my nose ... I believe this is the first event I can remember.

A second type of situation consisted of 'repisodes', that is, representations of repeated episodes (in the sense of Neisser, 1981), some situation that occurs repeatedly. One interviewee was asked for a situation making clear what determined when he watched television:

I: Which role does TV play in your life today? Could you please tell me a situation that makes that clear for me?

IP: Really, the only time when television has a certain relevance for me is New Year's Day, because I am so slain, that I can do nothing else but watch TV, well I have been doing this for years, spending New Year's Day in front of the TV.

A third type was historical situations, referring to some specific event. One interviewee referred to Chernobyl when he was asked for his most relevant experience with technology:

I: What was your most important experience or encounter with technology? Could you please tell me that situation?

IP: Probably, well, the reactor catastrophe at Chernobyl, because that has intrigued rather decisively the lives of many people, that made it clear for me the first time how much one is at the mercy of technologies.

Triangulation of data sorts in the episodic interview

In the episodic interview, the different types of questions aim at different sorts of data (narratives, argumentations, explication of concepts) in order to triangulate them. As in other interviews, the data produced in applying the method do not in every case or always meet the ideal concept of a 'situation narrative'. Applications of the method have shown that in the episodic interview not only these types of situations are presented, but also different sorts of data:

- *situation narratives* on different levels of concreteness;
- *repisodes* as regularly occurring situations, no longer based on a clear local and temporal reference;
- *examples*, which are abstracted from concrete situations, and metaphors, also ranging to clichés and stereotypes;
- the subjective *definitions* (of technology or health) explicitly asked for; and
- linked to them, *argumentative-theoretical statements*, e.g. explanations of concepts and their relations.

The episodic interview produces different sorts of data, which are located at different levels of concreteness and relation to the interviewee. It aims at social representations (see Flick, 1998; Moscovici, 1998) and thus a mixture of individual and social thinking and knowledge. In the episodic interview, moving back and forth between narratives of situations that the interviewees have experienced themselves and more general examples and illustrations, if they result from a narrative stimulus, is not seen as a loss of authenticity or validity (as in other forms of narrative interviews). Rather this complements the variety of data sorts making up social representations. Thus, episodic interviews may include the sorts of data represented in Figure 3.3.

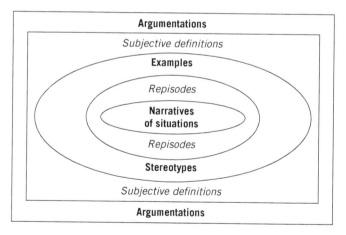

FIGURE 3.3 Data sorts in the episodic interview

The episodic interview is based on a triangulation on several of the levels that Denzin (1970) has suggested: different theoretical perspectives are linked to each other as well as the methodological approaches resulting from these perspectives, which then leads to different sorts of data.

EXAMPLES OF USING WITHIN-METHOD TRIANGULATION
Analyzing health concepts of health professionals

In what follows, an example of applying this strategy of within-method triangulation will be outlined, which has been mentioned before. The study 'Professionals' representations of health and ageing in home care for older people' (see Flick et al., 2003, 2004) focused on contents, relevance and, if applicable, changes in the concepts of health and ageing held by general practitioners and home-care nurses in two German cities. It could also inform about how far health as a leitmotif for professional practices has become part of the professional everyday knowledge of general practitioners and nurses.

The central research questions were:

- What is the specific concept of health in old age held by the professionals?
- Which dimensions of health representations are relevant for professional work with the elderly?
- What is the attitude of professionals towards health, illness prevention and health promotion for the elderly?
- What concepts of ageing do general practitioners and home-care nurses hold?
- What is the relation of these concepts with those of health?
- What is the relevance for one's own concepts of health and ageing in one's own professional practices?
- Are there links between the concepts of health and ageing and the professionals' training and professional experience?

Episodic interviews were conducted with 32 general practitioners and with 32 home-care nurses. In a short questionnaire, socio-demographic variables and structural data (training, professional experience, size of the institution, etc.) were collected. The analysis of the interviews showed that doctors' and nurses' health concepts were multi-dimensional, referred to somatic-mental well-being and were oriented towards the World Health Organization definition – also in rejecting it in the case of some doctors. Both professional groups defined health not only as the absence of illness, but saw it as a continuum. This showed that the concepts of public health and new public health (with a stronger focus on illness prevention and health promotion) had been adopted in the professionals' representations and their conceptual-semantic knowledge. At the same time, both professional groups did not only have a professional health concept. In the narratives of situations and examples, it became evident that health concepts were strongly influenced by personal and professional experiences in confrontation with illness. Experiencing their own illness and complaints had made them more understanding, empathic and engaged in their work with patients. Their professional training had for both groups no significant influence on their health concepts. For doctors as well as for nurses, it was evident that their concepts of health had changed as they had become more concrete and differentiated.

A change was not only described for health concepts but also for private and professional practices referring to health. These changes were influenced by the interviewees' private lives and by their growing older. The changes in professional practices referring to health were initiated by moving from hospital work to home-care nursing in the case of the nurses. For doctors they were initiated by the limitations of medical treatments. As a consequence, both groups reported a stronger integration of social and emotional aspects in treatment and care.

There were strong differences in how doctors and nurses described their private practices with regard to health. Many doctors presented themselves as very aware of health, whereas nurses in the majority reported that their practices were not really promoting their own health. This might be a reason why doctors confirmed an influence of their private health practices on their professional practices, whereas nurses saw private and professional life as separate in this respect.

Analyzing health professionals' concepts of ageing

Concepts of ageing were mostly differentiated for doctors and nurses and comprised negative as well as positive aspects referring to the somatic, psychological and social life situation. Both professions' concepts referred almost exclusively to very old people. The representation of age moved to the group more than 85 years old. It is interesting that hardly any positive body associations were mentioned. At the same time, we found certain differences in both groups' images of ageing, which was represented in their problems in defining age. Neither doctors nor nurses oriented their definition of 'old age' around the calendar age. They mentioned subjective criteria for being old (e.g. mental and physical decline, amplification of certain negative traits), which were more deficit-oriented. Both groups mentioned numerous examples of patients who did not meet these criteria; these people were not perceived as old. To some degree, age was seen as a signification of a form of living and of an attitude: 'You are as old as you feel and present yourself'.

Ageing played a role in the doctors' and nurses' private lives, as both groups mentioned their own ageing as linked to restrictions and complaints or talk about older relatives. When asked for the most important experiences of age in professional life, the doctors and nurses mentioned a number of positive examples of patients. Furthermore, they reported experiences with death and dying. It is noticeable that the interviewees hardly drew any consequences from their experiences in their private and professional lives and that they did not actively prepare for becoming old themselves.

Doctors and nurses described a change in their images of being old that was initiated by personal or professional experiences. Furthermore, they talked of societal changes. These experiences had made their images of age more multi-faceted and differentiated (see Walter et al., 2006).

Here we sometimes found significant differences between conceptual representations of health or ageing (at the level of conceptual-semantic knowledge) and the practices that were mentioned in examples and situation narratives (at the level of episodic-narrative knowledge), which became evident by triangulating both approaches (question–answer sequences and narratives). From the angle of quality in qualitative research, this strategy can provide different aspects of meaning, experience and relevance for the respondents and for the issue under study.

TRIANGULATION OF SEVERAL QUALITATIVE METHODS

Linking several research methods is the approach in triangulation that attracts most attention in qualitative research. On the one hand, this is embedded in a research approach – ethnography (see Chapter 4); on the other hand, this refers to combining qualitative and quantitative methods (see Chapters 5 and 6). Beyond that, more generally, this refers to combining different methods from different research approaches, but within qualitative research (see Figure 3.4). This will be outlined next.

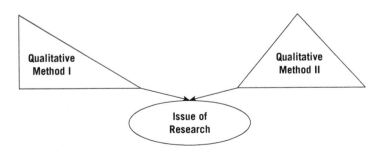

FIGURE 3.4 Triangulation of different qualitative methods

Here, we can again distinguish the use of triangulation for extending the knowledge of an issue or for mutually assessing results. In both cases, triangulation of different methods should start from different perspectives or at different levels: 'What is important is to choose at least one method which is specifically suited to exploring the structural aspects of the problem and at least one which can capture the essential elements of its meaning to those involved' (Fielding and Fielding, 1986, p. 34). This can be realized by combining methods that focus on the – everyday, expert or biographical – knowledge of participants, with methods that are addressing the observable – individual or interactive – practices of members. If we take up this **indication** for triangulation, it does not make much sense to combine two forms of interviews in one study, because they both may address different aspects of knowledge but will not go beyond the level of knowledge in collecting data. This would be the case if interviews were complemented by a method like observation or an analysis of interaction. Focus groups also use an extended interactive context for collecting data and thus are also methods operating at a different level than single interviews. The same is the case if we combine methods of analyzing visual materials with interviews. In these contexts, some of the problems that will be discussed later (see Chapters 7 and 8) arise: should the triangulation focus on the single case, should all cases be studied using the different methods or are two partial studies the better alternative, the results of which will be compared or combined later on? Likewise, the question arises of whether both methodological approaches should be applied in parallel or one after the other. For example, should interviews be conducted between, after or before an observation?

EXAMPLES OF BETWEEN-METHODS TRIANGULATION

In what follows, the technique of triangulating different qualitative methods will be outlined in two examples.

Interviews and conversation analysis

A study mentioned in Chapter 2 will be used as the first example. Here, counsellors' subjective theories of 'trust in counselling' were reconstructed and linked to their counselling practices. All in all, 15 counsellors – psychiatrists, psychologists and social workers – from socio-psychiatric services were included. The overall methodological strategy was oriented towards developing grounded theories in the field (according to Glaser and Strauss, 1967). A core aspect to be revealed in this strategy is the participants' knowledge of the phenomenon. Reconstructing the participants' subjective theories pursues this aim. The starting point is that people in everyday life – or in their professional practice – develop stocks of knowledge that are structured similarly to scientific theories. This knowledge is partly implicit, partly explicit. Research makes a **subjective theory** completely explicit by reconstructing it.

A second aspect that should be focused on in the discovery process was how trust is produced in counselling practices. This can be pursued in process analyses of consultations. They can also give information about the functionality of the subjective theories, as a form of expert knowledge, for practice and routines. A triangulation of both perspectives does not only have the aim of a mutual validation of their results. It should also catch the phenomenon under study in its complexity from different angles. If we want to reach this goal, the methodological approaches should be located at different ends of the range of qualitative methods. According to Fielding and Fielding (1986), such a triangulation should in one way focus on the meaning of the issue for the participants. This was the purpose of reconstructing counsellors' subjective theories. In a second way, the triangulation should analyze the structural aspects of the problem, which was pursued in (conversation) analyses of consultations.

Accordingly, this study triangulates two perspectives: on the one hand, a subjective intentional, reconstructive perspective looking for the meaning of a phenomenon (like trust) for the individuals in their (professional) practices; on the other hand, a structural-interactionist and interpretive perspective is taken, which focuses on structural aspects of a phenomenon like trust as part of social practices. Therefore, activities and statements are contextualized in social interaction patterns. They describe the processes in the organization of conversations, and how they can be understood from the outside, with the perspective of the interactive process, and not from the inside with the perspective of the participant. Intentions and actions of the individual (counsellor or client) are seen as accounts that can be analyzed in the context of the process and of the common production of what is going on. This aim was pursued through analyzing consultations according to conversation analysis principles (see Rapley, 2018).

This systematic triangulation of perspectives was employed at two levels:

- First, at the level of the single case to answer the question of whether relations between a counsellor's subjective theory and a consultation he or she had had with a client can be found. This shows functionality and action-relevance of the single subjective theory for counselling in the examined context.

- Second, at the level of comparative analyses: comparative systematization of the course of counselling shows regularities. If subjective theories are to be functional for those forms of talk and counselling, they must contain representations of those regularities found in the different courses of talk. In this way a set of categories can be developed out of one source of data (consultations), which can be used for interpreting the other source of data (subjective theories). Based on these findings, the entity of examples can be interpretively evaluated in the last step.

These methodological approaches are put into concrete terns as follows. Subjective theories are captured in a semi-structured interview. The interview guide focuses on various areas like the definition of trust, the relation of risk and control, strategies, information and *a priori* knowledge, reasons for trust, its importance for psycho-social work, institutional conditions, and so on. Among others, the questions in Box 3.2 were used for these purposes. The interviewee's statements are afterwards visualized, structured and communicatively validated – with him or her – by using the so-called structure-laying technique (according to Groeben, 1990). In the interview we find a statement like

Trust is made more difficult if the contact with the client comes about in an urgent situation and the counsellor (as social worker) always has in mind to observe if any strange, suspicious facts appear because of which he or she has to present the client to the physician in the team.

From this, the excerpt from a subjective theory in Figure 3.5 results.

BOX 3.2 EXCERPTS FROM THE INTERVIEW GUIDE FOR RECONSTRUCTING A SUBJECTIVE THEORY

- Could you please tell me briefly what you relate to the term 'trust' if you think of your professional practice?
- Could you tell me what are the essential and the decisive features of trust between client and counsellor?
- There is a proverb, 'Trust is good, control is better'. If you think of your work and relations to clients, is this your attitude when you approach them?
- Can counsellors and clients reach their goals without trusting each other?
- Will they be ready to trust each other without a minimum of control?
- How do people who are ready to trust differ from people who are not willing to trust?

(Continued)

(Continued)

- Are there people who are more easily trusted than others? How do those trustworthy people differ from the others?
- Are there activities in your work that you can practise without trust between you and your client?
- If you think of the institution you work in, what are the factors that facilitate the development of trust between you and your clients? What are the factors that make it more difficult?
- Does the way people come to your institution influence the development of trust?
- Do you feel more responsible for a client if you see that he or she trusts you?

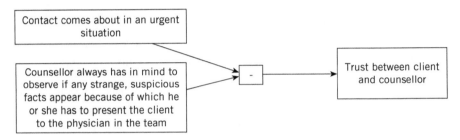

FIGURE 3.5 Excerpt from a subjective theory of trust

The second methodological approach in this study is to record (first) consultations that the counsellor interviewed before had with clients and to apply conversation analysis to them. Analyzing the opening situation should reveal, first, how a situation of counselling is produced and how a relation of trust is built up with the client. This allows extrapolating developmental patterns of such situations and deviations from such patterns. The following extract documents the beginning of a consultation that was done by the social worker (B) just mentioned with a client (K):

→**B:** Hmm, well, your grandfather came to us (K: yes), huh, he seemed to be very worried about you?

K: Yeah, I was feeling quite bad

B: Yes, what was the matter at that time?

K: In May, (.) you know, I drank too much a couple of days in a series and then I was feeling soo bad, because of the circulation (B: hmm), well everything, what you-, break out of sweat (B: hmm) raving of the heart, uuuh, burning eyes and everything, anyhow, and I didn't feel like laughing at all

→**B:** And then your grandfather also said, uh, well (.) your family doctor had said, meanwhile you are in a very urgent danger of death. Do you have an urgent organic-

K: Well, well, danger of death

B: complaints?

K: not really, ne? (B: hmm) There's just my fear, if I carry on that way, that still might come, (B: hmm) and that must not really happen, you know, I don't lay any stress on this (B: hmm) and therefore it's kind of a thing about drinking in my case.

B: How did it begin?

In the interventions marked by an arrow, the counsellor does not act according to the usual scheme – which could be shown across the consultations that were analyzed and also in similar studies before. According to this scheme, the consultation would start with exploring the problem from the client's point of view. In contrast to this, the counsellor first clarifies other aspects – the information she received from a third party (the grandfather). This deviation from the routine can be explained with the excerpt from the subjective theory in Figure 3.5: the third party, the grandfather, gave hints that there is an acute situation with possible endangerment for the client. The counsellor has to clarify this first in order to decide whether or not to present the client to the physician in the team. Only then can she start the consultation with the client in a traditional way and begin with the client's point of view ('How did it begin?') and build up a trustful relation.

In this example, the triangulation of both methods and of the data and results produced by both provides a complementary perspective at the level of the single case. In other examples, it provides divergent perspectives at this level. Divergent perspectives are particularly instructive as they raise new questions, for which we should seek theoretical or empirical answers (see also Flick, 1992, for this). Seen more generally, in comparing subjective theories, it could be shown beyond the single case how they represent the tasks and demands revealed by a comparative analysis of several consultations. Seen the other way around, a comparative analysis of the consultations shows the (for example, institutional) limitations of applying the subjective theories in professional practices.

Interviews and focus groups

The second example is our study of professionals' concepts of health and ageing that was mentioned before. In addition to within-method triangulation, different methods were also combined. Selected results from the single interviews were fed back and discussed in focus groups (see Barbour, 2018). These groups were organized in the two cities for the interviewed physicians and separately for the nurses. A main topic was the relevance of the health concepts we found for the participants' professional practices and a discussion of the consequences that should be drawn from them on how to plan these practices. The aim was to advance a transfer of the results into the health system and its practices. At the same time, new data were collected in these focus groups. Here, the stress is laid on the interactive aspect of collecting data: 'The hallmark of focus groups is the explicit use of the group interaction to produce data and insights that would be less accessible without the interaction found in a group' (Morgan, 1988, p. 12).

Focus groups are used as a stand-alone method or in combination with other methods (surveys, observations, single interviews, etc.). Morgan (1988, p. 11) sees focus groups as useful for: orientation in the field, generating hypotheses from participants' statements, developing interview schedules or questionnaires, and obtaining participants' interpretations of results.

In our study we principally pursued the last aim mentioned by Morgan. The general relevance of focus groups is characterized as follows: 'First, focus groups generate discussion, and so reveal both the meanings that people read into the discussion topic and how they negotiate those meanings. Second, focus groups generate diversity and difference, either within or between groups' (Lunt and Livingstone, 1996, p. 96). In the focus groups, we could not feed back the whole range of our results from the interviews due to time and capacity reasons. As an entry point into the discussion, we chose the barriers against prevention, health promotion and a stronger orientation towards health in the participants' own medical or nursing practice, which had been mentioned in the interviews. For all focus groups in this study, we planned a common concept of how to proceed, which was adapted to the number of participants and to the group dynamics in each case. For moderating the groups, we used the meta-plan technique. The groups should run though the following steps:

- *Entry.* In the beginning, the research project was briefly presented and the methods were described. Then selected results were presented that referred to the doctors' and nurses' attitudes towards prevention for older people and how to realize it.
- *Presentation of the barriers.* In the next step, we presented the barriers mentioned in the interviews on the side of the patients, of the professionals and of the health system. Sometimes, relatives (interfering with care and making professional care impossible) and the surroundings (a missing elevator) had been perceived as barriers. In the focus of the following discussions the barriers were on the side of the patients and of the professionals.

- *Ranking.* After answering questions for a better understanding, we asked the participants of the focus groups to rank the barriers. By nominating the three barriers they individually felt to be the most important ones using meta-plan techniques, we produced a ranking for each group. This result was taken as a starting point for the following discussion of how to solve these problems.
- *Discussion.* As a stimulus for the discussion of the results, we used the questions 'Do you find your position represented in the result? What is missing for you?'. The discussion about solutions to the problems mentioned here was initiated with the question 'Do you have any suggestions for how to overcome the barriers?'
- *Result.* At the end of the session, the main results of the discussion were noted on meta-plan cards, documented as a commonly produced result on a flip chart and finally validated with the group.

Focus groups as an additional methodological step allowed the participants to evaluate, comment on and criticize the results from the interviews. This produced additional results at a different level – group interaction instead of single interviews. In addition to interviews and focus groups, other materials (curricula and journals) were analyzed in the study.

TRIANGULATING METHODS IN THE CONTEXT OF ADVANCING QUALITATIVE RESEARCH

Within-method triangulation aims at a systematic combination of several approaches in the context of one method. Its background should be the combination of different theoretical approaches. Its result will be the existence and connection of different sorts of data. Data triangulation according to Denzin may refer to using various existing data. Within-method triangulation can be used for different purposes. In our examples, the central aim was to use the knowledge potential of two approaches systematically and to complement or extend them mutually. This should open up complementary perspectives on the issue in the experiences of the interviewees: a concrete process perspective, revealed in narratives of situations ('when I first used the computer'), etc., is complemented by an abstract description of a state ('for me, a computer is …'). This allows the showing of different facets of how interviewees subjectively deal with an issue. Thus, at the abstract level of general relations, a female French information engineer repeatedly argued about the gendered barriers for women in approaching computers or technologies in general. In the concrete situations, she recounted a consistent success story of how she mastered resistant machines and complicated situations.

Within-method triangulation, as the examples should have shown, is when various approaches in one method are used systematically and are theoretically well founded. A pragmatic inclusion of open questions in a questionnaire consisting of closed questions is not a typical example of within-method triangulation, nor is the acceptance of narrations in an interview, which is generally based on question–answer sequences.

The triangulation of several qualitative methods makes sense if the methodological approaches that are combined open up different perspectives (e.g. knowledge and practices), introduce a new dimension (e.g. group interaction versus single interview), start from different levels (e.g. analyzing documents or images versus verbal data) or if the potential gain of knowledge is systematically extended compared to the single method. Additional knowledge can be used to confirm (validate) the results coming from one method. Even more instructive will be methodological triangulation, if it provides complementary results, that is, a broader, more comprehensive or even complete image of the issue under study. Particularly challenging are divergent results coming from different methods demanding additional theoretical or empirical explanation. Thus, methodological triangulation can provide a fuller picture of one issue (what do people think of something and how do they act in reference to it?). It allows comparison of the results of different approaches (do people act as they say they do or as they think one should do?) and it can extend the levels at which an issue is studied (knowledge, practice, institutional background). All these contributions can be made if different methodological approaches coming from qualitative research are combined explicitly in one method or by linking several methods.

A specific extension of within-method triangulation in qualitative research will be discussed in the following chapter, where the triangulation of several approaches within the research strategy of ethnography will be discussed. A special version of between-methods triangulation will be discussed in Chapters 5 and 6, where combinations of qualitative and quantitative research and mixed methods will be the issue.

KEY POINTS

- Triangulation can be applied within qualitative methods and between them.
- In both cases it allows different perspectives on an issue to be combined in one research design.
- This will produce different sorts of data, which can be analyzed per se or with respect to extending the insights provided by a single-method approach.

FURTHER READING

Triangulation of qualitative methods is covered in these texts:

Denzin, N.K. (1989) *The Research Act*, 3rd ed. Englewood Cliffs, NJ: Prentice-Hall.
Fielding, N.G. and Fielding, J.L. (1986) *Linking Data.* Beverly Hills, CA: Sage.
Flick, U. (2000) 'Episodic interviewing', in M. Bauer and G. Gaskell (eds), *Qualitative Researching with Text, Image and Sound: A Handbook.* London: Sage, pp. 75–92.

CHAPTER FOUR

TRIANGULATION IN ETHNOGRAPHY

CONTENTS

CHAPTER OBJECTIVES

After reading this chapter, you should know:

- that ethnography as a research strategy often comes close to the idea that using several methods contributes to the quality of a study;
- that triangulation in ethnography is often used implicitly, but that there are also ways of using it explicitly in the field; and
- that here again triangulation contributes to quality by combining different perspectives on one issue rather than by a pragmatic combination of methods.

Whereas the preceding chapter dealt with triangulation in or between qualitative methods (like interviewing), we now come to a field where implicit and explicit triangulation of methods has been seen as a feature of qualitative research for some time. In what follows, we will address the use of triangulation in ethnography in principle and in examples from research practice.

FROM PARTICIPANT OBSERVATION TO ETHNOGRAPHY

Ethnography as a research strategy (see Coffey, 2018; Atkinson et al., 2001) has increasingly replaced participant observation (see Lüders, 2004a, p. 222) – at least concerning the methodological discussion. For participant observation, Denzin has already mentioned the triangulation of different methods as a feature: 'Participant observation will be defined as a field strategy that simultaneously combines document analysis, interviewing of respondents and informants, direct participation and observation, and introspection' (1989, pp. 157–8). Accordingly, we find a number of works in the literature about qualitative research in the 1960s and 1970s that are devoted to the combination, differences and relative strengths and weaknesses of participant observation and interviews as part of it; see, for example, Becker and Geer (1960) but also Spradley's (1979) suggestions for the ethnographic interview, and more generally, the studies of Glaser and Strauss (1967).

Triangulation has attracted special attention in methodological discussions in ethnographic research. Marotzki (1998, p. 52) mentions the combination of participant observation and interviews as typical of Malinowski's research. The Marienthal study of Jahoda et al. (1933/1971) combined several (qualitative and quantitative) methods in an ethnography without mentioning the term triangulation explicitly.

For more recent educational ethnography, Marotzki (1998, p. 47) sees the triangulation of methods and of data sorts as the rule, whereas a methodological discussion about it remains rather cautious. Methodological triangulation has become relevant for ethnography in general. Lüders (1995, p. 32) sees ethnography developing into a research strategy that includes all possible and ethically legitimate options for collecting data.

In this context, Hammersley and Atkinson's (1983) considerations are of special relevance: they highlight that data collection in ethnographies refers to accounts of different participants involved, which for them also includes the researchers' perspectives. Beyond triangulating data sources and different researchers, they mention 'technique triangulation' as a third form. Their aim in this is to use the comparison of data collected using different methods to control the 'validity threats' that are inherent in every technique. Their understanding of triangulation seems to be strongly informed by a technique orientation and claims for validation.

Hammersley continues to use such a concept of triangulation, which emphasizes a validation perspective, in later publications (1996, p. 167). At the same time, Hammersley and Atkinson discuss several problems linked to such a concept. They emphasize that in data triangulation it is not possible to combine different data per se (Hammersley and Atkinson, 1983, p. 199). Rather, a relation between the data is constructed in such a way that we overcome limits of single data types. They also emphasize that it is less the convergence than the divergence of data sorts that is instructive. According to this understanding, in comparing a person's knowledge and practices, triangulation should aim less at finding confirmation that the person acts according to his or her previously analyzed knowledge. Rather it should focus on the question of how to explain discrepancies between knowledge and practices theoretically. That is why Hammersley and Atkinson call their approach 'reflexive triangulation' (1983, p. 200).

IMPLICIT TRIANGULATION IN ETHNOGRAPHY: HYBRID METHODOLOGIES

Methodological approaches that are necessary for realizing the aims of a study are triangulated in ethnography, even if the term triangulation is not always explicitly used. At the end, we often have not only a mutual validation of results coming from single methods but an extension of the knowledge potentials about the life world under study. As the different methods like observation and interviewing are mostly combined ad hoc in a situation of prolonged participation, we can also talk of an *implicit* triangulation in ethnography. Characteristic of ethnographic research is the flexible use of different methodological approaches according to the situation and the issue in each case. Not only is the use of the methods adapted to the situation, but perhaps also the methods themselves (Lüders, 2004a, p. 226). In later publications as well, it is especially this flexible use of all possible sources of information as data that is suggested for ethnography, without explicitly spelling out the combination of specific methods or a formalized combination of specific sorts of data: 'One must engage in what Denzin called triangulation, checking everything, getting multiple documentation, getting multiple *kinds* of documentation, so that evidence does not rely on a single voice, so that data can become embedded in their contexts, so that data can be compared' (Rock, 2001, p. 34). For Amann and Hirschauer (1997, p. 19) ethnography is characterized by a – compared to other qualitative research strategies much stronger – methodological imperative of the field over the discipline (methods, theories, etc.). They want to make clear that it is not the preferences for specific methods resulting from a certain disciplinary tradition or discussion – for example, in sociology – that should determine the researchers' encounter with the field under study (and with the empirical 'material'), but the methodological needs that are produced by the field, its features and peculiarities. For the 'data materials' produced in such encounters, with their characterization of the data in ethnographic research, the authors come rather close to the concept of data triangulation. They emphasize the need to liberate ethnography from methodological constraints as obstacles against immediate personal contact to the field. If we look at the research practices that have been published according to this conception – for example, in the collection by Hirschauer and Amann (1997) – it becomes evident that this liberation from methodological constraints refers to three points: in entering the field, in deciding which concrete methodological approaches to take to the interesting practices and members, and in how rigorously the methods are applied. Narrations are often part of the data, but not necessarily as a result of consequently applying narrative methods. Nevertheless, ethnographers use methods and normally a variety of methods (mostly observation, recording, interpretation and interviewing) in combination. Accordingly, Knoblauch (2004, p. 356) speaks of ethnography as being particularly predestined for '**hybrid methodologies**' – the use of complementary methods addressing different aspects of issues. What is practised in such a hybrid methodology is nothing else but a concept of methodological triangulation, which goes beyond the idea of correcting and validating. However, it remains implicit, as not much attention is paid to a systematic combination of methods.

EXPLICIT TRIANGULATION IN ETHNOGRAPHY: THE PRECEPT OF TRIANGULATION

Beyond such a pragmatic or implicit use of triangulation in ethnography, we also find a growing discussion of explicitly combining specific methodological approaches. Some authors (such as Marotzki, 1998; and Schütze, 1994), even talk of a precept of triangulation as

the honest commitment to combine different methods of data collection and analysis, different data sorts and theories according to the research question and area in such a methodologically controlled way, that a research design results that allows to provide credible and reliable knowledge about the person in his or her socio-cultural context. (Marotzki, 1998, p. 52)

For Marotzki this precept of triangulation refers to the combination of participant observation and interview technique or, for Schütze (1994), to the combination of narrative interviews and analyses of protocols and documents of interaction processes. Schütze (1994, p. 235) sees ethnographic reports, original texts, narratives, and expert interviews and focus groups as sorts of materials for ethnographic research. For Schütze, this precept of triangulation above all is relevant in the context of using ethnographic research and results as a starting point for training (in social work) and consultation with clients (by social workers).

Practical considerations of resources and impositions for participants or fields are mentioned in this context. A critical discussion of the concept and application of triangulation in ethnography comes from Kelle (2001). She breaks down an abstract methodological discussion of triangulation to concrete questions of research practice in ethnography. First of all she underlines that methods cannot be taken offhand out of the research perspective in their background: 'Various procedures cannot ... be thought and brought together at arbitrary parts of the research process, but only applied in parallel' (2001, p. 193). Then she highlights that junior scientists often carry out the research projects. They 'have to acquire theories and methodological tools not infrequently in the course of such a project'. Therefore 'using several methods cannot per se be seen as better than concentrating on one methodological procedure' (2001, p. 193).

For the first point of her critique, it could be noted that the approach of a systematic triangulation of perspectives (see Chapter 2) addresses this question. Here, the aim is not the simple combination of methods at arbitrary parts of the research process but the combination of methods by taking into account the theoretical methodological research programme from which they come. The second point Kelle makes addresses the precept of triangulation formulated by Schütze and Marotzki, which raises the question of when a triangulation is indicated (see Chapter 9 for this).

More instructive is Kelle's approach to discussing questions of triangulation of research perspectives for concrete problems of collecting and documenting research materials. Kelle discusses these questions against the background of combining participant observations (documented in observation protocols) and interaction practices (documented in audio or video recordings). The background of her discussion is the distinction between reconstructive and interpretive methods (Bergmann, 1985; see also Chapter 2). In this distinction, a quasi-genuine access to the reality under study is attributed to the latter, whereas the former is attributed to a (re-) constructive filter. As Kelle shows, both forms of documentation are characterized by selective filters. In one form, the subjective condensations of the observer or in producing the field notes are the origin of the filter. In the other form, the limited reach of the recording machines in time, in focus and in what can later still be transcribed is the reason, especially when the medium of recording lacks selectivity in what is recorded. More generally, Kelle demonstrates that any form of collecting and communicating data is a constructive effort and that no method allows a genuine access to what is studied. According to Kelle, any method produces reductions in the complexity of what is under study, but she holds at the same time: 'These reductions are necessary, if you want to be able at all to make a specific statement about the area of research, because it is not possible to put all aspects of a complex practice "under the microscope" at the same time' (2001, p. 202).

Kelle provides good arguments for a reflexive approach to triangulation in ethnography. She proposes reflecting the possibility of linking methods at the level of the concrete application and especially at the level of the forms of documentation necessary for each method. This is an important suggestion in the discussion of triangulation in general. The same is the case for her advice that an application of different methods needs a profound knowledge and training in each of these methods. However, it is less convincing to turn this argument against using triangulation in general. In another paper (Dausien and Kelle, 2003), she argues for combining ethnographic and biographic perspectives and expects that this will deepen ethnography and descriptions and enlarge the perspective of biographical research.

In summary, such approaches of explicit triangulation in ethnography outline ways to complement the limitation of ethnography – the here and now of what can be observed – by enlarging the perspective beyond situations of observation into a biographical framework or more generally to knowledge used by the participants in the observed situations.

EXAMPLES OF TRIANGULATION IN ETHNOGRAPHY
Communitization processes in sports

A first example of using triangulation in ethnographic research comes from a study of the processes of community formation in traditional and new sports (Gebauer et al., 2004). For this study, several fields were selected in which the sport practices in traditional sport (handball as a team sport in clubs), in new forms of sport (inline hockey in public places) and in mixtures and combinations (**triathlon**), and their social representations (Flick, 1998; Moscovici, 1998), were analyzed empirically. Explicit triangulation was used here, as ethnographic methods of an extended participation and observation (see Coffey, 2018) in the field, where new sports like inline hockey were played, were combined with the use of episodic interviews with single participants in additional appointments outside the observation. The first approach enabled the researchers to analyze practices and communications. The second illustrated the meaning of the sport and the scene for the individuals.

The most consistent approach is to apply the triangulated methods to the same cases (see Chapter 8). Persons observed in a field are (all) interviewed. This allows a case-oriented analysis of both sorts of data and comparing and linking the different methodological perspectives for the single case. In addition, comparisons and links can be established at a higher level also. Patterns resulting from comparisons in one sort of data (process patterns of play in sports) can be linked to patterns coming from the other data form (emphases and blind spots coming up in all interviews in one field or in general). Sampling decisions have to be taken only once, as for both sorts of data the same selection of cases is used.

The disadvantages are that the load for an individual participant in the study is relatively high: to participate in observation and to give an interview is more than is usually expected from participants in a study. At the same time, the danger of dropout rises, as everyone who refuses either the interview or the observation is 'lost' for the whole study. Finally, observation in open spaces (like sport 'scenes' such as inline hockey in a town square) is confronted with the problem that perhaps so many persons are observed at the same time that not all of them can be interviewed, without going beyond the resources of the study. Therefore, triangulation again is possible only in a very limited way for the single case, but it can also start from the level of datasets.

In using triangulation in datasets single methods are applied independently in the first step and produce a set of observational data and a series of interviews. Both are analyzed for their commonalities and differences. Triangulation refers practically to the results of both analyses and puts them into relation. As a practical problem, the question arises of how to ensure the comparability of the samples to which the different methods were applied.

Methodological triangulation in our example was oriented on three research perspectives:

1. Analyzing practices, interactions, codes, artefacts and gadgets, and forms of movement in different forms of organizing games in each sport.
2. Analyzing social representations of each sport.
3. A sociological analysis of social localizations and memberships.

Triangulation of methods

The following methods were triangulated: ethnographic participant observations and descriptions of the field for each sport; episodic interviews with the members focusing on representations of the sport and of their own and group-specific practices; and a questionnaire focusing on the social background and affinities for localizing the members in the social sphere.

Ethnographic participant observation was understood as a research strategy (according to Lüders, 2004a) for analyzing concrete contexts and human development in a cultural surrounding (Jessor et al., 1996). A special interest was developed for clothing, rituals and symbols, which are used for marking social territories. Ethnographic participant observation can be used for analyzing social frames (Goffmann, 1974) by capturing aspects of space, time, noise (music, signals), objects and devices, rules, norms, codifications, and so on. Research questions in this study focused on social organizations and memberships in the particular field. Are members more oriented towards trainers or role models or more towards peer groups? Does the sport support individualization or not? Which performative acts, self-presentations and movements are typical for each form of sport? Which codes, rituals and symbols are used to indicate members in the community of each sport? (see Coffey, 2018).

Phases of observation

In making ethnographic participant observation work, we can distinguish three phases (according to Spradley, 1980, p. 34). (1) Descriptive observation in the beginning is for orientation in the field and provides unspecific descriptions. It is used to grasp the complexity of the field as comprehensively as possible and to develop more focused research questions and perspectives. (2) In focused observation, the perspective is increasingly narrowed to the processes and problems that are particularly relevant for the research question. (3) Whereas selective observation towards the end is more intended to find further evidence and examples for what was found in the second step, such as types of practices or processes. Particularly for the second and third phases, an observation manual was developed with key aspects like description of space, structure of time, contents of training, descriptions of persons, ways and structures of communication, posture and gestures, rules, norms and habits.

Structure of observational protocols

The resulting protocols of observation had the following structure: day, date, period of observation; name(s) of observer(s); keyword for the main event; situation on arrival; list of events in keywords; chronological description of the observations; description of conversations; the researchers' own feelings and reflections on their activities in the field; first interpretations, questions, hypotheses; and open questions and hypotheses for the next observation.

One problem in ethnographic participant observation is often how to limit and select situations of observation in which the phenomenon under study becomes 'visible'. That is why more or less comprehensive interviews with participants are often used. In our case, training for triathlons can be principally localized for the swimming, in that (a group of) athletes can be systematically observed. The other activities (running, cycling) are hardly accessible for observation, as they are practised by single actors and not at defined places. Such activities are more accessible in interviews.

Episodic interviews in sports

Accordingly we did episodic interviews in this study, in which question–answer sequences were triangulated with narratives. With the first questions, the interviewees were invited to explain their subjective definition of the issue of research, for example: 'What is the meaning of triathlon for you? What do you link to the word "triathlon"? What characterizes the atmosphere of triathlon for you? Could you please tell me a situation that makes that clear for me? Could you please try to remember the situation in which you decided to do triathlon as a sport and tell me that situation?'. Instructive for the analysis is the concrete situation, which is narrated in what is reported as happening in it, but also the selection taken from the multitude of possible situations for elucidating one's viewpoint. The next step was to clarify the role or relevance of the issue for the interviewee's everyday life. For this purpose, interviewees were asked to relate a typical daily routine in order to highlight the sport's relevance in it ('Please tell me how your day went yesterday and where and when triathlon played a role in it'). The interviewer could pick up certain aspects for probing from this multitude of situations. In the next step, the interviewees were asked to explain their personal relation to central aspects of the research issue for their life in general, for example: 'What is the role of sport in your professional life; your professional education? Could you please tell me a situation for this?'. In the end, interviewees were asked to talk about more general aspects of the issue and to unfold their personal views ('On what does it depend, if someone decides on this sport and continues to do it? Could you please give me an example of this?'). This aimed at extending the perspective. As far as possible, the interviewer would try to link the general statements with the interviewee's personal and concrete examples in order to let possible contradictions and discrepancies become visible. As in other interviews, interviewees would be given the chance to add something they felt was missing in the interview at the end.

The episodic interviews for all the sports in this study included narrative stimuli and questions for the following areas: subjective meaning of the sport; relevance of the sport in everyday life; social affinity or distinction through this sport; and a final, evaluative part (see Chapter 3).

The empirical material for interpretation, which resulted from both methodological approaches in our study, included on the one hand case studies for single actors based on interviewing them and field descriptions of the fields under study, and on the other hand, more general analyses on the basis of the empirical material (see Gebauer et al., 2004). In what follows, short excerpts from a field description and from a case study will be presented.

Triathlon as a field

In Berlin, we find about 1,000 people organized in triathlon clubs. Triathlon competitions have been organized here since the middle of the 1980s, so triathlon is a rather young form of sport. In the competitions we observed, the relation between male and female participants was consistently around 3 to 1. It was interesting that the men, who started in five-year classes, were dominated by 35–45-year-olds. The actors themselves classified triathlon mainly as a higher-level sport and clearly dissociated themselves from popular sports such as handball and above all soccer. In triathlon, in contrast to many conventional club sports, which are concentrated on an architectonic, specifically designed, special space like a gym or a stadium, we have to speak of spaces (using the plural) of this sport. Already the different spaces where triathlon is practised demonstrate its position as a hybrid between traditional and post-conventional sport. In indoor swimming pools, the swimming training is held at fixed times, often together with members of swimming clubs and under their organisational regimen. Diverse and continuously newly defined tracks for cycling and running at the edge of town are used individually or in small groups.

The triathlon meetings and competitions take place in special places. Only the swimming pools and the locations of the competitions are accessible for an ethnographic observation. Only here do the athletes gather and only here does the culture of the ethnicity under study constitute in a locally concrete way. Only here does the field 'triathlon' have clear physical and local boundaries. In other words, triathlon is not only a transgression at the levels of achievement and time limits, but also a local extension of traditional sport practices. In some sense, the sport practices start in the swimming pool, at a clearly defined location, in order to burst out beyond the boundaries and to transgress them. The practice of triathlon reproduces in itself the changes from conventional sport, which is limited and tied to specific local ghettos and fixed times, to post-conventional sport practices, for which it is constitutive to break these limitations and to claim spaces for sport practices that have so far been spared this.

In triathlon, the swimming training is the 'fixed point, where you always meet', as one female participant states. Here, the athletes meet at fixed hours of training. They are locally put together, but they are seldom amongst themselves, but mostly with other club swimmers and – during the public hours – with leisure swimmers. In order to work against a possible mix-up with ordinary swimmers, the athletes distinguish themselves here again with their outward appearance (short, often blond-dyed hair, often tattoos, men's legs being shaved, everyone is wearing a noticeable watch) and behaviour: extended exercises of stretching and warming up, training schedules that are displayed beside the pool and consulted after each course, often only ephemeral hellos and good-byes, and finally the – very individually operated – long periods of training.

In one of our field notes, we noted accordingly:

Most athletes in triathlon seem indeed – as was announced by the trainer beforehand – to be concentrated very strongly on themselves. In the indoor pool, there was hardly any contact among them. What about the greeting and farewell sequences, what happens in the dressing rooms? During my observation, I had the feeling that they are not irritated at all to be observed by a stranger. My feeling of distance, or dissociation, seemed to be 'reproduced' in the relation between the athletes and to the trainer. The athletes act as a community of individualists already in the indoor swimming pool. (field note – triathlon)

Competitions are central to triathlon. Only here can the athletes pass the swimming, cycling and running courses in an immediate sequence, which are practised separately in the training. This requires special locations. Their regular use has to be restricted during the competitions. Therefore, triathlon competitions have to be registered with the police and other agencies. Streets have to be closed to traffic. Bicycle stands, changing facilities, organization and catering stands have to be erected. Triathlon practices do not integrate in the everyday forms of using public spaces, as, for example, inline hockey does. Rather they transfer such spaces into special areas for sport for a short time (and with problems and organizational effort). For the participants, competitions have the character of special events. Here, the community of the athletes becomes visible to itself. Here, the single protagonists meet. At these special locations and mostly at exceptional times (often very early on Sundays) they can experience themselves as a community. At the competitions, the athletes – together with trainers, family members and friends – are their own audience. External spectators would be, as a protagonist puts it, 'bored to death' by such competitions, because the proceedings in the competitions, the athletes' fights against themselves and their rivals, can be displayed to viewers only with difficulty.

To compensate for this performance deficit, which is constitutive for triathlon, bigger competitions of nationwide interest are produced as events with an extended supporting programme. The athletes appreciate such events for their special atmosphere; they accept long journeys, expensive hotels and high fees in return for being part of the triathlon at Ratzeburg or the 'Iron Man' at Roth in Germany. Triathlon as a field has formal organizational structures of clubs and associations in common with traditional sport. However, the explicitly instrumental relation of the athletes to such organizational forms is characteristic of triathlon. Often membership is only seen as relevant for having access to and the opportunity of training in the indoor pools. Many athletes only use the swimming training in the context of the club and practice the other two disciplines (cycling and running) by themselves or – if the individual schedules can be coordinated – with a training partner. In contrast to most sport in clubs, competitions are seldom run as competitions between clubs or club teams. Rather it is the individual competition in well-differentiated age groups defined by the association that is central. The instrumental relation to and individualist erosion of the social form of the club in triathlon become most evident in the missing festivities and meetings that are typical of sport clubs and that serve to cultivate and maintain sociability. For such a club life beyond the sporting practice, often the localities like club houses, regularly frequented pubs, and so on, are missing in triathlon. Protagonists who have taken voluntary club positions repeatedly complain about the missing sociality of the athletes. The other members continuously state that the club, beyond the functional aspects mentioned before, 'actually does not have any relevance for the contacts among us', as one participant in our study puts it.

Subjective meaning of triathlon

Observation and field descriptions allow practices and social relations that are characteristic for the field to be revealed. The subjective meaning of the sport and the individual representations of community linked to this sport are more accessible in the narratives in an interview. Therefore, some excerpts from the analysis of an interview with a female protagonist from the field of triathlon will be presented next. At the time of the interview, the interviewee is 27 years old and looks back on an almost lifelong career in sports: 'I began as a six, seven year old with track and field … I was drawn in by a family who all do track and field.' After many steps she finally moved from athletics to triathlon, which she had practised for three years 'properly', that is, training every day, regular participation in competitions and in club structures, and in which she invests a lot of energy: 'Well, I am not a high-level athlete in a strict sense but upper mass sports section, I would say'. It is noticeable in this interview that the interviewee – in contrast to other interviewees – hardly mentions any positive aspects of this sport and its protagonists in her description of triathlon. She describes the athletes as obstinate, rigid single fighters, who are 'not open' and 'often not so funny and happy'. They permanently ignore themselves and their own feelings and prove incapable of building up more intense, mutual social relations. According to her description, it is not the ones looking for the particular, intense and extravagant who practise triathlon but only those who cannot help doing it. Thus the membership in this sport is based less on a selection and decision, which could always be revised again ('There are never such people who completely stop and start again. Such people feel the inclination again, well a friend of mine, she thinks, well somehow it was quite a nice time, but she'd never start again'). Rather it is based on a personal trait of the protagonists: 'Either the people are athletes from their personal type, I'd say, and then they stop for a little while and then continue.' The negative stylization starts with refusing the Greek and seemingly antique word creation 'triathlon' and the pretension it carries:

before I started to say: 'I do triathlon', I have actually always said, when asked, what sport I do, it almost was the case today, although I have been doing triathlon for two three years, that I said, well, I run, cycle and swim. But this triathlon per se has a strange meaning, somehow … well for me this is a little strange concept.

In an emphatically prosaic understatement, she prefers her sport to be understood as 'running, cycling and swimming'; she does not like to use the strange label 'triathlon', which aims at distinctiveness and exclusivity.

In the further development of the interview, two related aspects are the main grounds for her negative image of triathlon and of the athletes linked to this sport. For her, athletes are characterized by 'not much knowing themselves, never doing anything according to their feelings ... they permanently ignore themselves'. The self-discipline invested by the protagonists to manage the enormous amount of training in triathlon ('You have often to convince yourself extremely and you need quite a lot of self-discipline for this sport') has a flavour of masochism for the interviewee. The athletes debar themselves from traditional pleasures and lust, in order to obtain satisfaction from a sometimes extreme 'self-torture'. This masochist relation to oneself even becomes evident in the way in which the 'athlete per se' uses a sauna, as the following excerpt from one of our interviews documented:

you sit in the sauna, actually sauna should be something nice and relaxing, and the last time I suddenly recognized, I came into the sauna, I thought, I fall backwards out through the door again. This guy had turned it to 100 degrees [Celsius], sits and scrubs himself with a horse brush, and I think, that's unbelievable. The more the better, the more torture the better. (interview excerpt)

The interviewee's presentation of these self-techniques, which are characterized by discipline, rigidity and escalation, includes an ambiguity that is rooted in the second core aspect of the negative image of triathlon she outlines: although the athletes permanently ignore themselves, they are permanently concerned with their own interests in an almost pathological self-centredness. This extreme self-centredness, which permanently misses the own self, obstructs any reference to others. They are 'amazingly individualistic ... everyone works for him or herself', they 'do their own thing ... and it does not matter for them, whether you are there or not'. As mentioned before, they are 'not open' and therefore not only unable to integrate into a community built on solidarity and reciprocity, they are also unable to have an intense love relationship:

I mean, that has something to do with a relation, and that is of course not found by persons who need, let's say, so much warmth and cordiality and much affection. Well, this is expressed rather extremely now, but I think that in particular athletes then again have fewer problems in their relationships, which one actually expects, because the people who are in such a relation are not so demanding in the wish of being together. (interview excerpt)

This presentation shows a polarity that gives a contour to the interviewee's negative stylization of triathlon (and the athletes) against the background of her own self and world images. In her critique of the individualism of athletes, it becomes evident that she (as a sports club activist in particular) much appreciates orientations towards communities, cohesion and solidarity. In contrast to a life planned for the sport, in which rigid daily training programmes dominate every other activity, she draws a positive image of features and states like being relaxed, easy-going, all in all a nonchalant laissez-faire. This includes sometimes saying: 'Today, I don't feel like it, I'll lie in bed and watch TV' or 'to have a nice breakfast and see what the day will bring'. Only at the very end of the interview does she outline a positive aspect of her triathlon practice; however, it remains unclear whether this is a wish or a real experience of hers:

And that is so often what I miss so much. I often go to the training, because I think, well today the sun is shining, I am really keen now on driving around and watching the birds and simply to get out of the city and to rush along the forest cart roads and not because the training schedule says 90 minutes cycling now. And that is what I miss so often at the athletes, to look a little more at, what do I really want myself, yeah? That's all actually. (interview excerpt)

Triangulation of observation and interviewing

The triangulation of both approaches in ethnography shows, first, how the distinction in the field is put into practice in activities, attributes and forms of communication, as the situation in the indoor swimming pool shows. Furthermore, the role of formal processes of community building, of individualizing and informal forms of dissociation as practices in the field in constituting social relations and communities become visible. This reveals the social construction of community in this field. The ambivalences that are linked to this form of (missing) community for the actors and the biographical pathways that have led them there are only (exclusively or complementarily) revealed in the interview. Here, the contribution of the individual to the social construction of the field shines through. This reveals not only commonalities in the data and analyses resulting from both methodological approaches, but even more the discrepancies and different facets that become possible only after the triangulation of methods and research perspectives outlined here.

Homeless adolescents' health and illness

As a second example, I use our study about homeless adolescents' health and illness (see Flick and Röhnsch, 2007; Flick, 2011), which integrates the triangulation of several qualitative methods in an ethnographic approach.

Observing and interviewing homeless adolescents

The starting point was participant observation at major contact points and hangouts of street youth. The first focus was the life situation of adolescents, aged between 14 and 20 years, on the street. Then the focus was increasingly on how they managed health risks and on their health-related practices and interactions. The observations and the embedded informal conversations allowed identification of the topics for the subsequent more systematic interviews as well as possible interviewees. In the first part of the project 24 adolescents were recruited without considering their health situation or specific health problems. They were interviewed about issues such as how they entered street life, their family background, their health concepts and how they managed health risks in areas such as alcohol, drugs, eating and sexuality. The second part of the project focused on chronically ill homeless adolescents aged 14–25 years.

In the interviews, a lot of space was given to how they managed health risks – who was consulted in such a case, which experiences had been made with self-help, with support by their peers or with the utilization of medical or social work services and professionals. The interviews were episodic interviews. The narratives and statements were related to the observations, which were continued in parallel, to identify links and differences between both kinds of data. This can be demonstrated for the example of the utilization of physicians in case of health problems in the sub-sample of chronically ill adolescents. We could identify several patterns of utilization behaviour, in particular concerning physicians.

Seeing a doctor as self-evident

One example of this first pattern is Daniel[1], suffering from hepatitis C, with an amputation of his right leg and facing the threat of amputation of his left lower leg:

as long as the virus degree is not in an area, that you have to treat it, I don't have it treated ... it is controlled by the doctor and that is actually the most important thing you should do if you have this disease. (Daniel, 24 years)

Other participants in this pattern have neurodermatitis or allergies to dyestuffs and band-aids and strong skin irritations. These adolescents have no doubts about the relevance of the doctors' prescriptions. They see them as mandatory, so they keep appointments with doctors exactly. They are ready to invest time and money for

---

1 All names have been changed.

handing in prescriptions. Professionals' suggestions about how to deal with the disease are taken up, changing their illness behaviour. However, more extensive changes in daily routines are hardly realized.

Seeing a doctor as a distant option

Denise is an example of our second pattern. While other adolescents here have asthma, hay fever, obesity and alcoholism, she suffers from allergies to animal hair and milk and most evident in her daily life, extreme obesity. She refers to the allergic reactions on her skin, when she says:

If it is impossible to stand it, if my whole body is really full from head to feet and there is no part free of it at all, then I would go [see the doctor] … But it was not so serious so far. Lucky me. (Denise, 16 years)

These adolescents again have no doubts about their need for medical treatment. However, currently they do not seek or receive treatment. They postpone seeing a doctor as long as possible, and at the moment their symptoms are not urgent enough to make professional help necessary. Their lack of insurance is seen as an obstacle to using medical services. Also they see as an obstacle to medical treatment that they are living on the street.

The doctor as a risk

This pattern applies to a number of adolescents suffering from lactose intolerance, hay fever, hepatitis C, anorexia, unclear problems with the skeleton, neurodermatitis, cardiovascular problems, chronic bronchitis and asthma. Romy is 14 and suffers from chronic bronchitis. She describes her experiences:

I took many drugs in addition, drank alcohol and afterwards some aspirin or so because of my headache and all that did not really fit together and then I passed out. (Romy, 14 years)

She and the other interviewees to whom this third pattern applies express a strong distrust of any doctors. This has to do with experiences of feeling left alone when the diagnoses they were told produced a shock. In general they see doctors as incompetent. Another reason for their scepticism is that they experienced themselves as being treated like a layperson by doctors. Finally, they see treatments as experiments at their expense. And as Romy's statement shows, these adolescents experience treatment as risk rather than as help.

In our observations we found another pattern we labelled as 'fatalism':

Jan has fully developed AIDS. Asked about how he feels, he answers, it has to be OK, he still could get along with it, and now it was too late anyway to expect a substantial improvement, there is nothing that could be done for him anymore. He would attend the Homeless Doctor, she would provide him with painkillers and there is nothing else he still wants anymore. (observation A-22.02.2005)

Jan expresses a rather fatalistic attitude towards his disease and his further life. He does not expect treatment or improvement anymore but only pain relief. He disappeared from the field soon after.

The patterns we found are summarized in Table 4.1. This shows that the last pattern applies to half of our interviewees, although the patterns were found across the different diseases in our group.

TABLE 4.1 Utilization patterns of medical services

	Adolescents				
	Male	Female	Total		
Interpretive patterns	*N* = 6	*N* = 6	*N* = 12	Interview	Observation
Seeing a doctor as self-evident	2	1	3	×	
Seeing a doctor as a distant option	1	2	3	×	×
Seeing the doctor as a risk	3	3	6	×	

Table 4.1 also shows which patterns of dealing with health problems could be found in the observation protocols and which in the interviews. It also shows how many of the interviewees it applies to, and which gender they are.

This excerpt from the findings should also demonstrate how the use of observations and interviews in this study could reveal differing aspects of the issue under study and of the research question.

Chronic illness may subjectively be experienced by those who are affected in different ways from the perspective when 'objective' or professional criteria are applied. In the next step, the subjective views of the adolescents were complemented by the external perspectives of people working in social and health services, who were working with chronically ill homeless adolescents. These people can be seen as experts in estimating the adolescents' situations, needs and problems. We analyzed the experts' views on the adolescents' need for support and which health care deficits might exist in supporting this target group. We included physicians and social workers who specialized in working with homeless people (not necessarily adolescents) or who worked in institutions for specific target groups (like hepatitis C patients) and thus might be relevant for our adolescents because of their diseases (see Table 4.2).

TABLE 4.2 Sample for the expert interviews

| | Experts | | |
| | Physicians | Social workers | Total |
Fields of work	$N = 5$	$N = 7$	$N = 12$
Basic service (social street work and surgeries for homeless people, general practitioners)	3	3	6
Medical and social assistance for specific groups (e.g. prostitutes, hustlers, hepatitis C patients, drug users)	2	4	6

When looking at what our experts say about deficits in the health care for homeless adolescents with a chronic illness, we find four areas mentioned (Table 4.3). Five experts mention particular sub-groups among chronically ill adolescents on the street who do not receive support. Here, migrants from Eastern Europe living illegally in Germany are mentioned. These adolescents could claim neither for appropriate housing nor for medical treatment. Seven experts talk about a lack of specific institutions or the professional knowledge necessary for appropriate support for the adolescents. In particular, the social workers complain about a lack of physicians visiting the adolescents at their meeting points to offer basic medical support. Doctors for the homeless, particularly working with people without insurance, do not really meet the adolescents' needs as the social workers say. Four social workers say that the existing health projects miss the adolescents' needs because of their structure or their way of working. Furthermore, the institutions are too specialized and networking among them is weak. Competition rather than cooperation is dominant and knowledge about what other institutions could contribute is limited.

should be better coordinated and linked ... Support for homeless people, institutions for people with addictions, for youth in general is available, but among these three areas there is hardly any coordination in the help that is offered. (social worker)

Beyond that, there are not enough services and people are not trained to work with homeless adolescents. These problems are complemented by the limited accessibility of health care for people without insurance or who do not have their papers with them. Only one doctor sees no deficits in the health care for homeless adolescents (see Table 4.3).

TABLE 4.3 Health care deficits seen by the experts

	Experts		
	Physicians	Social workers	Total
Health care deficit	$N = 5$	$N = 7$	$N = 12$
Lack of health care for certain target groups	3	2	5
Inappropriate way of working or structure of existing services	–	4	4
Lack of institutions or competence	3	4	7
Limited accessibility of health care	1	1	2
No deficit	1	–	1

Triangulation of observations and several interview forms: outcomes in this study

Triangulating the three approaches: observation, interviews with adolescents and interviews with experts can reveal different aspects of the phenomenon under study (health and illness of homeless adolescents). Observations give insights into individual and shared practices concerning health-relevant problems. Interviewing the adolescents allows access to areas that are not accessible for observation, and to more general assumptions, experiences and practices beyond concrete (observable) situations from the participants' point of view. Expert interviews provide assessments of the problems and life situations beyond the single case of an interviewed adolescent. All three levels of approaching the issue together reveal contradictions and differences but also overlaps in and additions to the perceptions and presentations of the problem.

IMPLICIT AND EXPLICIT TRIANGULATION IN ETHNOGRAPHY

Triangulation in ethnography is applied in varying forms and with varying consistencies. At some points it is seen as constitutive for the ethnographic attitude in the field, but is then applied mostly implicitly. At other points it is explicitly and consistently requested even in a precept of triangulation. Problems that are raised refer to the necessary skills for applying two (or more) methods. Thus, Kelle ends her paper with a sort of scepticism: 'In the methodological literature, it is often pretended that one could make use of different theoretical approaches and methods as if they were ready on the shelf' (2001, p. 206). Successful use of triangulation requires a high degree of theoretical skill, and calls for working into the different approaches to be triangulated. But is that not the case for how ethnographic research practice has been described by authors such as Lüders, Atkinson, Hammersley or Rock anyway, even if the claim for triangulation is not made explicit? In ethnographic research practice, triangulation of data sorts and methods and of theoretical perspectives leads to extended knowledge potentials, which are fed by the convergences, and even more by the divergences, they produce.

As in other areas of qualitative research, triangulation in ethnography is a way of promoting quality of research. Often it is used more in an implicit than an explicit way. It is even more important than in other areas, as in ethnography quality issues are treated implicitly less than in qualitative research in general. As one indicator of this, we do not find a chapter addressing quality issues per se in the otherwise excellent handbook of Atkinson et al. (2001). Good ethnographies are characterized by flexible and hybrid use of different ways of collecting data and by a prolonged engagement in the field. As in other areas of qualitative research, triangulation can help to reveal different perspectives on one issue in research, such as knowledge about and practices with a specific issue.

OUTLOOK

In this and the preceding chapters (2 and 3), triangulation was outlined with regard to current strategies, approaches and examples in the realm of qualitative research. One reason for this focus is that the discussions about triangulation since the 1970s were mainly related to qualitative research and concentrated on this type of research. However, authors such as Kelle and Erzberger (2004), but also Bryman (1992) or Greene (2007), see a space for triangulation in the combination of qualitative and quantitative research as well, although the latter two authors are examples of those who define a very limited space for it in this context – mainly the confirmation of qualitative results with quantitative methods (or vice versa). The major part of the literature in this context is now devoted to concepts of mixed methods research. In the next chapters, we will address combinations of qualitative and quantitative research and start by outlining mixed methods as an approach to such combinations.

KEY POINTS

- Triangulation can be used in ethnography as a strategy for extending the approach of a concrete research project.

- As methodologies in general remain rather unspecific and are mainly linked to attitudes more than to explicit strategies in ethnography, the use of triangulation often remains implicit here also.
- Using triangulation in ethnography more explicitly can be more fruitful in extending insights in the field under study.

FURTHER READING

These authors address ethnography from the angle of using different methods in the framework of the ethnographic approach, and at the same time give an interesting introduction to ethnography as such:

Coffey, A. (2018) *Doing Ethnography* (Book 3 of *The SAGE Qualitative Research Kit*, 2nd ed.). London: Sage.

Flick, U. (2018) *Designing Qualitative Research* (Book 1 of *The SAGE Qualitative Research Kit*, 2nd ed.). London: Sage.

Hammersley, M. and Atkinson, P. (1983) *Ethnography: Principles in Practice.* London: Tavistock (2nd ed. 1995, Routledge).

Lüders, C. (2004) 'Field observation and ethnography', in U. Flick, E. von Kardorff and I. Steinke (eds), *A Companion to Qualitative Research.* London: Sage, pp. 222–30.

Rock, P. (2001) 'Symbolic interactionism and ethnography', in P. Atkinson, A. Coffey, S. Delamont, J. Lofland and L. Lofland (eds), *Handbook of Ethnography.* London: Sage, pp. 26–39.

CHAPTER FIVE

WHAT IS MIXED METHODS RESEARCH?

CONTENTS

CHAPTER OBJECTIVES

After reading this chapter, you should understand:

- how and when a triangulation with quantitative research can be used to advance qualitative research;
- that a simple combination of methods tends to neglect the methodological and often theoretical differences among both approaches; and
- how mixed methods research gives a concrete and practical shape to the idea that combinations of qualitative and quantitative approaches can be fruitful.

The idea that quantitative research can be used to advance qualitative research is still in the air. It has become prominent again in particular in the context of discussions about mixed methods (Tashakkori and Tedlie, 2003a) and about all sorts of **evidence-based practices** (see also Morse et al., 2001; or Denzin and Lincoln, 2005, for this). Both discussions have critical potential for qualitative research, as they tend to question the independence and value of qualitative research on its own. Despite this, a reflected use of quantitative approaches can contribute to qualitative research. For implementing this suggestion, it seems necessary to outline how such a combination can be realized, and which pitfalls and strategies should be taken into account in such a combination. Methodological discussions were marked for a long time by argumentations with sharp distinction, which highlighted the differences in the theoretical, epistemological and practical-research starting points of qualitative and quantitative research. In the USA, this discussion was even labelled the 'paradigm wars' (Lincoln and Guba, 1985). This argumentation about distinctions has led to a sharpening of the methodological profile of qualitative research and to a growing diversification in the field. It has also had the consequence that quantitative standardized research was relatively unimpressed and has pursued its own topics and internal methodological issues. Both research areas – qualitative and quantitative research – have remained and developed relatively independently alongside each other.

THE RELEVANCE OF LINKING QUALITATIVE AND QUANTITATIVE RESEARCH

Several trends in overcoming a strict separation of qualitative and quantitative research can be noticed. A starting point is the notion, slowly being accepted, of seeing qualitative and quantitative methods as complementary and not as rivals

(Jick, 1983). Such trends aim at linking qualitative and quantitative research. Following Bryman (2004), we can more generally distinguish two levels at which the relation of qualitative and quantitative research – and thus an option for, or the impossibility of, their triangulation or for mixing them – is discussed. At the level of 'epistemology', the fundamental incommensurateness of both approaches is focused on, sometimes referring to the specific paradigms in each case. In the 'technical version' of the discussion, these differences are seen, but not as impossible to overcome or to take into account. The focus is rather on the usefulness and contribution of one approach for the other.

Wilson (1981, pp. 43–4) has outlined a systematization of aspects that characterize social situations, with which they can be analyzed and which provide clues for selecting qualitative or quantitative methods and their combination. He distinguishes in this context 'the objectivity of social structure', existing independently of the actions of the individual and which influences actions via norms and rules. The 'reference to commonly shared stocks of knowledge' makes it possible to understand and localize the other and his or her action in the situation. The 'context-dependency of meaning' has its rationale in the fact that the specific meaning of an action or statement is different according to each specific context and can only be understood in this context.

Another form of combining qualitative and quantitative research can be realized at the level of the data, when we transform the data from one strategy into the other – from qualitative into quantitative data and vice versa. In the programmatic of 'mixed methodology research' the transformation of one form of data into the other is advocated (see below), but without making concrete suggestions for how to do it.

In a similar way, Hammersley (1996, pp. 167–8) distinguishes three forms of linking qualitative and quantitative research. *Triangulation* of both approaches stresses the mutual validation of results and not so much the mutual addition of knowledge potentials. *Facilitation* highlights the supporting function of the other approach in each case; for example, one approach provides hypotheses and ideas for carrying on the analysis with the other approach. And finally, both approaches can be combined as *complementary* research strategies. The 11 ways of integrating quantitative and qualitative research Bryman (1992) identified have been discussed earlier in this book (see Chapter 1).

Brewer and Hunter (1989) have presented an approach of 'multi-method research'. They are interested in a 'synthesis of styles' and start from four basic methods of empirical research that can be combined in different ways. These basic methods are field research (the approach of Glaser and Strauss, 1967), surveys (using representative questionnaires), experimental methods and nonreactive measurements. As a leading concept, they use triangulation for combinations with reference to Denzin (1970). However, they talk of 'triangulated measurement' in the logic of mutual validation of results (Brewer and Hunter, 1989, p. 17). They discuss their approach of triangulation or multi-method research in applying it to all phases of the research process. All in all, they cleave too much to the logic of standardized research, in which they simply want to integrate field research.

Johnson and Turner (2003) pick up the question of linking qualitative and quantitative methods in the context of 'mixed methodologies', but do not develop specific approaches. A standard example used here again is to include open questions with free text answers in an otherwise standardized questionnaire. Seen the other way round, we can then also describe the documentation of quantitative information (like age, income, number of children, years of professional experience, etc.) or certain scales in an otherwise open interview as a form of integrating qualitative and quantitative methods of collecting data (see Flick, 2014a, Chapter 24, for the use of documentation sheets for collecting such data in the context of episodic interviews). Finally, data analysis in both cases will include the linking of qualitative and quantitative approaches: in the first case the coding of the free text answers, in the second of the numbers received. More elaborate here is the use of time, speed and frequency rates in observations of movements and activities, as in the study of Jahoda et al. (1933/1971).

For analyzing qualitative data, Kuckartz (1995) describes a method of coding of first and second degree, in which dimensional analyses lead to defining variables and values that can be used for classifications and quantifications. Roller et al. (1995) outline a method of 'hermeneutic-classificatory content analysis', which integrates ideas and procedures of objective hermeneutics (see Reichertz, 2004) in a mainly quantitative content analysis. In a similar direction goes the transfer of data, analyzed using programs like **ATLAS.ti**, into SPSS and statistical analyses. In these attempts, the relation between classification and interpretation remains rather fuzzy.

From a more general point of view we can conclude that in most cases one approach is dominated by the other and integrated in the latter in a fairly marginal way (for example, we often find a small number of open questions among a multitude of closed questions in a questionnaire), which is why these examples seldom represent a triangulation of qualitative and quantitative methods. The development of really integrated qualitative/quantitative methods remains a problem to be solved. Concrete suggestions for how to integrate both approaches in one method, which really could be called 'triangulation', are still awaited.

MIXED METHODS: CLAIMS AND CONCEPTS

Beyond that, we often find the integration of qualitative and quantitative methods or mixed methods (Tashakkori and Teddlie, 2003a) and triangulation (Kelle and Erzberger, 2004) as concepts for linking both approaches. Which label is chosen in each case shows the different claims linked to each approach. As the current discussion about combining qualitative and quantitative research or about complementing qualitative research by using quantitative approaches is dominated by the use of 'mixed methods' as a label and approach, we will outline this approach here, before later coming back to a more integrative perspective.

Mixed-method methodologists are interested in facilitating a pragmatic combination of qualitative and quantitative research, which is intended to end the paradigm wars. Tashakkori and Teddlie (2003b, p. ix) declare this approach to be a 'third methodological movement', quantitative methods being the first and qualitative methods the second movement. A methodological elaboration of this approach aims at the clarification of concepts ('nomenclature'), of designs and applications of mixed methodology research and questions of inference in it. Using the paradigm concept in this context, two more or less closed approaches are assumed, which again can be differentiated, combined or rejected, without diving into the concrete methodological problems of linking both approaches. The concept of triangulation is rejected by several of the authors (e.g. Sandelowski, 2003; Tashakkori and Teddlie, 2003c), not least to promote their own concept of mixed methodology research.

Claims of mixed methods use

Claims linked to mixed methods research are outlined and 'a truly mixed approach methodology (a) would incorporate multiple approaches in all stages of the study (i.e., problem identification, data collection, data analysis, and final inferences) and (b) would include a transformation of the data and their analysis through another approach' (Tashakkori and Teddlie, 2003b, p. xi). These are very far-reaching claims, especially if we consider the transformation of data and analyses (qualitative in quantitative and vice versa – see Chapter 6).

Definitions of mixed methods

A number of suggestions have been presented for how to define mixed methods over the years (see also Creswell's most recent suggestion discussed in Chapter 1). In the context of evaluation research, Greene et al. (1989) suggested a rather pragmatic definition of mixed designs 'as those that include at least one quantitative method (designed to collect numbers) and one qualitative method (designed to collect words), where neither type of method is inherently linked to any particular inquiry paradigm' (p. 256). Greene (2007) later suggested a definition of mixed methods as a way of looking at multiple ways of making sense of the social world. More comprehensive is the suggestion coming from Creswell and Plano Clark (2007, p. 5), who include philosophical assumptions and the use of qualitative and quantitative methods as essentials in their definition. As some kind of consensual concept a definition of mixed methods comes from Johnson et al. (2007, p. 123), which has been established and used in many methodological works as a point of reference, again stressing the combination of qualitative and quantitative approaches as essential in mixed methods research. Greene (2008) outlined a methodology for what she calls 'mixed methods social inquiry' for which she sees four domains: philosophical assumptions and stances; types of inquiry logic or methodology, such as logic, quality standards, writing forms; guidelines for practice procedures and tools; and socio-political commitments.

These earlier suggestions for defining mixed methods research are characterized by the intention to locate practical issues of a specific research concept (the use of qualitative and quantitative methods in one or another form of combination) in a broader research programme including references to theories and epistemologies. More recent suggestions go more strongly in practical directions, when Creswell, for example, defines a limited number of 'core characteristics of mixed methods', among which the collection and analysis of quantitative and qualitative data and methods, in a mixed methods design, and: 'sometimes, framing of the design within a philosophy or theory' are important (2015, p. 3).

Paradigms as orientation for creating a new approach

The methodological discussion about what mixed methods research is and how it is distinct from and goes beyond what already existed in the social (or educational) sciences was often linked to the notion of paradigms. Johnson and Onwuegbuzie (2004) spell out this idea exemplarily. They start from the notion that 'there are many important paradigmatic differences between qualitative and quantitative research' (2004, p. 15). The authors refer to the so-called 'paradigm wars' (2004, p. 14) and outline two ways out of this situation: first to define mixed methods research as a third paradigm, and second to try to reconcile the earlier controversies by linking mixed methods research to pragmatism (2004, p. 14). This linkage has been further pursued by Morgan (2007) among many others. The consequence of this argumentation is that in many cases combinations of specific qualitative and quantitative methods are no longer the reference points in the methodological writings but rather the combinations of the qualitative and quantitative paradigms – or of Qual and Quant (e.g. Morse, 2014).

This rather brief overview is intended to show in which contexts the combination of qualitative and quantitative approaches is currently being discussed. In what follows, I will try to spell out a little more what contribution can be expected here from triangulation as understood in our context.

EXAMPLE OF MIXED METHODS RESEARCH

In what follows, an example of mixed methods research will be briefly discussed.

Coping with cancer in the family

Schönberger and von Kardorff (2004) studied the challenges, burdens and achievements of cancer patients' relatives in a combination of a questionnaire study with two waves of surveys (189 and 148 relatives and 192 patients) and a number of case studies (17, of which seven are presented in more detail). The research questions for both parts of the study were characterized as focusing on 'the experience of burdens, on individual and partnership coping, on integration in networks and the evaluation of the services in the system of rehabilitation' (2004, p. 25).

In addition, the authors conducted 25 expert interviews in the hospitals involved in the study and eight expert interviews in after-care institutions. The participants for the case studies were selected from the sample for the survey. The criteria for selecting a couple for a case study were that: 'The couples should share a flat, the partner should not suffer from a severe illness, and the ill partner should be in a rehabilitation clinic or after-care centre at the time of the first data collection' (p. 95). Furthermore, contrasting cases to this sample were included: people living by themselves, couples with both partners being ill, or cases in which the patient's partner had died more than a year ago (2004, p. 95).

The quantitative data were first analyzed using several factor analyses and then in relation to the research question. In the presentation of the questionnaire results, 'a link to the case studies is made, if their structural features match findings from the questionnaire' (p. 87) or if they showed exceptions or a deviance. All in all, the authors highlight the gains in differentiation due to the combination of surveys and case studies (2004, p. 201) as they made it possible to discover the links between subjective meaning-making (in the illness narratives), the decisions and coping strategies and styles which were reported and the latent meaning structures … Above all, the structural moments and the learned capacities to integrate the situational elements in one's own biography and in the one shared with the partner were important. (2004, p. 202)

This study can be seen as an example of combining qualitative and quantitative methods (and data), in which both approaches were applied consequently and in their own logic. They provide different aspects in the findings. The authors also show how the case studies can add substantial dimensions to the questionnaire study. Unfortunately, the authors do not say which findings from the questionnaires were helpful for understanding the single cases, or what the relevance of the quantitative finding was for the qualitative results.

● KEY POINTS

- Mixed methods research builds on the idea that combinations of qualitative and quantitative approaches can be fruitful for studying specific issues.
- A number of suggestions for developing a conceptual grounding of mixed methods research by defining its characteristics as a design and as a research programme have been made.
- The trend in this discussion moves away from outlining a methodology towards defining core characteristics on the level of methods and designs.

■ FURTHER READING

In these sources, the combination of qualitative and quantitative research is discussed without falling into euphoria about mixing methods on a pragmatic level, and so they can give insights for the discussion of using triangulation of qualitative and quantitative research in the context of quality issues for qualitative research:

Bryman, A. (1992) 'Quantitative and qualitative research: further reflections on their integration', in J. Brannen (ed.), *Mixing Methods: Quantitative and Qualitative Research*. Aldershot: Avebury, pp. 57–80.
Creswell, J.W. (2015) *A Concise Introduction to Mixed Methods Research*. Los Angeles, CA: Sage.
Flick, U. (2014) *An Introduction to Qualitative Research*, 5th ed. London: Sage, Chapter 3.
Greene, J.C. (2007) *Mixed Methods in Social Inquiry*. San Francisco, CA: Jossey-Bass.

CHAPTER SIX

DESIGNS, METHODS AND DATA IN MIXED METHODS RESEARCH

CONTENTS

CHAPTER OBJECTIVES

After reading this chapter, you should understand:

- which designs are discussed and can be used in mixed methods research;
- how the mix of both approaches can be put into concrete terms in combinations of methods;
- how this can be realized by linking qualitative and quantitative data;
- that many examples focus on linking the results of both approaches and what characterizes this; and
- that quality in qualitative research can be promoted by integrating quantitative parts in the research not only at the level of quality assessment but also by adding more and different aspects of knowledge about the issue of research from each of the approaches.

QUALITATIVE AND QUANTITATIVE DESIGNS

The development of integrated designs comprising qualitative and quantitative research has been discussed in various contexts. Rather early on, Miles and Huberman (1994, p. 41) suggested four basic designs including the parallel use of both approaches and various sequences of qualitative to quantitative methods or vice versa (see Figure. 6.1).

These suggestions on the one hand cover much of the variation in more recent discussions about how to design mixed methods research. On the other hand they can be seen as a starting point for later proliferations.

Parallel use of qualitative and quantitative research

In the first design suggested by Miles and Huberman, qualitative and quantitative are used in parallel. In the second design, a continuous field observation provides a basis for different waves of surveying. Their third design starts with collecting qualitative data (e.g. in a semi-structured interview), which is followed by a survey as an intermediate step, before the results from both steps are elaborated and validated in a second qualitative phase. In their fourth design, a field study complements and deepens the survey results from the first step, which is followed by an experimental intervention in the field to check the results from both steps (see also Patton, 1980, for similar suggestions for mixed designs).

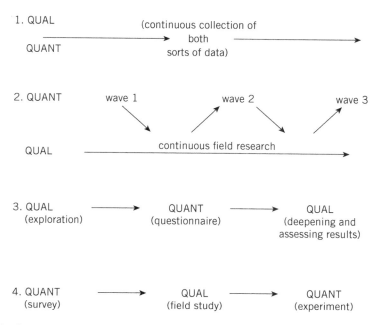

FIGURE 6.1 Research designs for the integration of qualitative and quantitative research (adapted from Miles and Huberman, 1994, p. 41)

Sequential combination of qualitative and quantitative research

Without necessarily reducing one approach to being inferior or defining the other as the main approach, a study may include qualitative and quantitative methodologies in different phases of the research process. Barton and Lazarsfeld (1955), for example, suggest using qualitative research for developing hypotheses that will afterwards be tested by quantitative approaches. Therefore, these authors are repeatedly taken as a starting point for defining a subordinate, merely exploratory role for qualitative research or for dissociating one's own position from such an understanding. However, in their argument, Barton and Lazarsfeld do not focus only on the limits of qualitative research (compared to quantitative), but they explicitly see the strength of qualitative research in the exploration of the phenomenon under study. Following this argument, qualitative and quantitative research is located at different stages of the research process. These authors discuss explicitly various strengths of qualitative research, which they see in the discovery of relevant problems for research, in providing hints of phenomena that cannot be directly observed, and in constructing descriptive systems, preliminary classifications and systematic typologies.

Exploring an issue under study is one of several functions of qualitative research. Even if Barton and Lazarsfeld (1955) see most of the functions of qualitative research they discuss as localized 'before quantitative research', qualitative research is seen as a necessary precondition of quantitative research and less as a preliminary step, which can basically be left out. Rather, Barton and Lazarsfeld discuss a series of examples to show that certain insights cannot be found or adequately analyzed without qualitative methods. According to them, qualitative research can reveal possible connections, reasons, effects and even the dynamics of social processes, and it is only qualitative research with an unstructured collection of data that can reveal this. At the same time, they see the innovative part of the research beyond tables of a few variables defined in advance and in qualitative data collection. Following their reasoning, qualitative and quantitative research is localized in different phases of the research process. Qualitative research should be positioned more at the beginning of dealing with an issue, but can also be used for the interpretation and clarification of results from statistical analyses. Thus, Barton and Lazarsfeld make suggestions for linking both approaches, which are similar to what Bryman (1992) proposed more recently (see Chapter 1).

Mixed methods designs

In his systematization of research designs in qualitative and quantitative research, Creswell (2003) also refers to integrated designs and distinguishes three forms:

1. Phase designs, in which qualitative and quantitative methods are applied separately one after the other, no matter in which sequence. Such designs can include two or more phases.
2. The second form is named 'dominant/less dominant' design and is mainly committed to one of the approaches and uses the other only marginally.
3. Mixed methodology designs link both approaches in all phases of the research process.

In the context of the mixed methodologies approach of Tashakkori and Teddlie (2003a), Creswell (2003) and Creswell et al. (2003) suggest a more elaborate version of designs linking qualitative and quantitative research. They see the mixed methods design as being a design in its own right in the social sciences (Creswell et al., 2003, p. 211).

Their matrix for determining a mixed methods design is an interesting suggestion. The authors use the term 'triangulation' in the context of a design named as 'concurrent triangulation'. According to their categories this design is characterized by a parallel collection of qualitative and quantitative data (implementation). The priority is preferably equal, but can be for either quantitative or qualitative data. Integration comes with the phase of interpretation of results or in analyzing the data. The theoretical perspective is perhaps explicit (pp. 224, 229).

Creswell and Plano Clark (2011, pp. 65–8) discuss a number of decisions to be taken in choosing or developing a mixed methods design. These discussions are about the priority of qualitative or quantitative strands, about the timing (parallel or what comes first) and about where and when the mixing of the approaches is planned exactly (e.g. during data collection, analysis or interpretation of results).

These actually rather simple dimensions used for describing a seemingly rather complex process of decisions become much more obvious if they are linked to and taken for a concrete issue to be studied. But for Creswell and Plano Clark they are first the basis for presenting a number of prototypes of major designs for mixed methods research. The convergent parallel design links both approaches in the step of interpretation of findings. The explanatory sequential design uses qualitative methods for better interpretation of quantitative findings. The exploratory sequential design uses qualitative findings for further interpreting what a quantitative approach has shown. The embedded design means that the other approach is included (before, during or after) in the first approach design – e.g. qualitative elements in a quantitative study. The transformative design goes beyond these types of methodological logic and is characterized by the idea that mixed methods research is done to change a situation or conditions. Finally, the multiphase design is a combination of several studies – for example, first a qualitative, then a quantitative and finally a mixed methods study about the same issue (see Creswell and Plano Clark, 2011, pp. 69–72). These suggestions have been widely published by Creswell and co-authors, and have been debated and become a dominant issue in the methodological discussion. Authors such as Hesse-Biber (2015) and Guest (2013) even worry about the trend to set up typologies of designs for mixed methods research, which suggest that researchers only have to decide which of these designs they should apply to their study without any longer asking whether a mixed methods approach fits at all (or not) to what they want to study. And finally, the 'which design to select?' issue is quite dominant, and in Creswell and Plano Clark's (2011) textbook all issues regarding methods of data collection and analysis are discussed from that angle.

Integrated longitudinal designs

Kluge (2001) goes one step further and describes 'integrated panel designs', in which several waves of qualitative interviews and repeated quantitative surveys for one research question are combined in order to study changes in viewpoints and interpretive patterns of the participants in a longitudinal perspective. The aim here is first to test how far the qualitative results can be generalized by the quantitative results (2001, p. 41). At the same time, the first approach is seen to be addressing the actors' perspectives, whereas the second studies social structures. Central for the methodological integration is that it contributes to an integration of the results (2001, p. 44; see also Kelle and Erzberger, 2004).

Research designs integrating qualitative and quantitative research methods can be classified according to the sequence of methodological approaches, to the weight given to each approach, their function, and the theoretical and methodological reflection of the combinations. Here we can distinguish the combination of methods for extending the knowledge potentials of research and for a unidirectional or mutual assessment of the results. A reciprocal addition in the methodological perspective on the research issue is assumed here. The addition comes from a complementary compensation for weaknesses and blind spots in the single methods. However, the different methods remain standing side by side; their point of intersection is the research issue. Whether the methods are used at the same time or one after the other is less relevant than that they are used on an equal footing in the project.

LINKING QUALITATIVE AND QUANTITATIVE METHODS

Beyond such design issues, the linking of qualitative and quantitative methods is the second core problem in mixed methods or similar ways of combining both types of research. However, a brief look at textbooks on mixed methods research reveals a rather limited interest in how to do data collection. As said before, Creswell and Plano Clark (2011) look at this issue only through the lens of their design typology. Greene (2007) does not have a chapter on data collection and concentrates on data analysis. *The Handbook of Mixed Methods* in its second edition (Tashakkori and Teddlie, 2010) comes without a chapter on data collection, whereas the first edition (Tashakkori and Teddlie, 2003a) has one chapter (Johnson and Turner, 2003) with a very general overview of data collection strategies in mixed methods research and a strong focus on questionnaires and interviews. This lack of interest in how to collect data and which data collection strategies should be mixed (and which maybe should not) may be an explanation for why Bryman (2006a) found in his study about mixed methods research practice that most mixed methods studies were done with a rather limited array of methods, mainly the combination of interview, questionnaire and a cross-sectional design.

To link qualitative and quantitative methods in the data collection step, integrative approaches have been discussed as well. Kluge (2001, pp. 63–6) describes four variants of integrating qualitative and quantitative methods of data collection: surveys can inform the formulation of an interview guide; life course charts resulting from survey data can be used in the interviews; statements from interviews can be turned into survey items; and survey results can be clarified in interviews.

For analyzing data, Kluge refers to the option of integrating quantitative data in the computer-assisted analysis of qualitative data (e.g. with ATLAS.ti or **NVivo**; see also Gibbs, 2018), or using interfaces to SPSS. Finally, she mentions quantitative techniques (cluster analysis) for analyzing qualitative data to develop typologies (Kluge, 2001, p. 74).

LINKING QUALITATIVE AND QUANTITATIVE DATA

Morgan (1998) suggests a classification of approaches of linking qualitative and quantitative research, referring mainly to the level of data collection. He organizes his classification first around the 'priority decision' – that is, which method is in the foreground during data collection, which one is subordinate – and around the 'sequence decision' – that is, which sequence is chosen.

Transformation of qualitative data into quantitative data

Attempts to quantify statements in open or narrative interviews come up repeatedly. Observations can be analyzed regarding frequency also. The frequencies with which categories are filled can be counted and the numbers in different categories can be compared. Counting specific features in transcripts or observation protocols can be a way to transform qualitative data from content analysis into nominal data, which can then be computed using statistical methods. Hopf (1982) criticizes a tendency in qualitative research to convince readers of research reports with arguments based on a quantitative logic (e.g. 'five out of seven interviewees said', 'the majority of answers referred to') instead of looking for a theoretically based interpretation and presentation of results. The argumentative pattern criticized by Hopf can also be seen as an implicit transformation of qualitative data into quasi-quantitative results. In the course of this transformation, a de-contextualization of information is undertaken – for example, when the frequency of a certain statement is isolated from the specific contexts in which it was done and regarded separately.

Transformation of quantitative data into qualitative data

The inverse transformation normally is more difficult, as a re-contextualization of singular data would be necessary. From questionnaire data, the (meaning) context of the single answer can hardly be reconstructed without explicitly using additional methods, like complementary interviews with a part of the sample. While analyzing frequencies of certain answers from interviews can provide additional information for the interpretation of these interviews, we need new data sorts (interviews, field observations) to be collected and added to explain why certain patterns of answers come up more often in a survey.

LINKING QUALITATIVE AND QUANTITATIVE RESULTS

Links between qualitative and quantitative research are often established for the results that both have provided. Accordingly, Kelle and Erzberger (2004) focus in their more general works on linking qualitative and quantitative research mainly on the level of results. They distinguish three alternatives: qualitative and quantitative results can converge, be complementary or contradicting. For all three alternatives, the same questions and problems come up in principle. How far was the specific background of both empirical approaches (in collection and analysis) taken into account? Do divergences perhaps result from a different understanding of reality and the issue in both (qualitative and quantitative) approaches? Should convergences to a (too) large extent not be a reason for being sceptical, rather than a simple confirmation of one result by the other? Finally, how far are both approaches and their results seen as equally relevant and independent insights, so that using the concept of triangulation is justified in this concrete case? How far is one or the other approach reduced to a subordinate role – for example, for only giving plausibility for the results of the other approach?

QUALITATIVE RESEARCH IN THE CONTEXT OF ADVANCING QUANTITATIVE RESEARCH

Linking qualitative and quantitative research has for a long time been discussed with a strong focus on mutual assessment of the quality of research and results (e.g. Jick, 1983). For example, we can use qualitative research for assessing the validity of data produced with a standardized instrument, as the following example may show.

Quality of life indices and interviews

To ensure and produce (again) **quality of life** is especially important when people live with a chronic illness. Then, which form and extent of quality of life can be achieved with certain treatments has to be assessed. Accordingly, research into health-related quality of life (Guggenmoos-Holzmann et al., 1995) is booming. Internationally and in different language areas, quality of life indices such as the **SF-36** (see Mallinson, 2002) are used. It is claimed that this instrument can be a generally valid index for assessing health-related quality of life. For the validity of this and similar indices, several questions are discussed that are interesting for our context. Most of the scales used in these indices have been developed in the USA. In transferring them to other language areas some validity problems become particularly visible, which arise in one cultural or language area if different populations with different cultural backgrounds inhabit it. Validity problems discussed in the context of quality of life indices are: How far can lists and items of physical and social functionality as included in quality of life indices be seen as equivalent to subjectively experienced quality of life? How far can they be transferred to the different social and local contexts in a society with the same validity? The item 'Are you able to walk five blocks every day?' may be an indicator for quality of life in American towns. In some areas of bigger cities, it rather indicates an overly venturesome behaviour. To translate into German 'five blocks' as a measure of the ability to move is quite difficult. Nevertheless, these items and scales are used for international comparisons of the quality of life in different countries.

Mallinson (2002) studied for the SF-36 the limits of the unambiguousness of questions for the respondents. This can be shown in the commentaries noted by participants in studies of quality of life at the margins of the questionnaires. These showed that the participants sometimes understood the questions completely differently from what the developers of the instrument intended. With the SF-36 interviewers want to find out how far respondents are restricted in certain everyday activities. For this participants are asked, for example:

The following questions are about activities you might do during a typical day. Does your health limit you in these activities? If so, how much? (Please circle one answer on each line).

G: Walking more than a mile – Yes limited a lot, Yes limited a little, No not limited at all

H: Walking half a mile – Yes limited a lot, Yes limited a little, No not limited at all

I: Walking 100 yards – Yes limited a lot, Yes limited a little, No not limited at all

Parallel open-ended interviews in Mallison's application of the SF-36 show that many participants in such studies have problems getting straight in their minds how far one mile or half a mile or 100 yards is:

IV: Can you walk half a mile?

IE: Where's half a mile?

IV: Say down to the garden centre, maybe a little bit further than that.

IE: I can walk down to the garden centre, but there's no way I could get back because it's up-hill and as soon as I, I can't walk up that hill so it depends which, if you're talking about on the flat, slowly, not talking or carrying anything. (Mallinson, 2002, p. 16)

Beyond such validity problems of items and scales in the questions that are asked, validity problems for the answers also arise. If the answer format is a **Likert scale** (very good; good; fair; poor; very poor; or in the example above: Yes limited a lot; Yes limited a little; No not limited at all), we can ask furthermore whether the distance between the single gradations in different languages is the same or not. This leads to the question of whether we can simply summarize or compare the circles around one of the alternatives without problems. In this example, combining an open (qualitative) procedure with a standardized (quantitative) method shows the limits of validity for statements collected using the second method.

In another direction, Silverman (1985, pp. 138–40) sees a way for assessing the **generalization** of qualitative results in adding quantifications. An alternative is the further contextualization of qualitative data by consulting quantitative data and an additional check on their plausibility. So our study of general practitioners' and nurses' health concepts showed that the interviewees hardly attributed any relevance to their professional training. Rather, professional experiences in their own practices and private experiences with health and illness are attributed the strongest influences. For contextualizing this result, we analyzed the curricula and training plans for the professional training of nurses and for medical sciences over a longer period for the quantitative relevance of topics like health, health promotion and prevention. In my study of counsellors' subjective concepts of trust in socio-psychiatric services in Berlin, it became evident that the dilemma between counselling and helping the client on the one hand, and the management of deviant behaviour on the other hand, determines the problematic nature of building trustful relationships in a particular way. In addition, the – purely quantitative – documentation of interventions was analyzed over a longer period. This showed first a shift in the focus of the work from placements of mentally ill persons in psychiatric wards towards counselling as an intervention for psychological problems. However, it also showed how large a part placements still have in the practices of the institutions. In these examples, quantitative data are used for contextualizing qualitative data and interpretations and to give them more plausibility.

Youth in survey and portraits

Another example is the Shell Youth Survey 2002 (Hurrelmann and Albert, 2002). Here, a representative survey of 2,515 adolescents between 12 and 25 years old using a standardized questionnaire is combined with more detailed or short portraits of 'committed' adolescents. The sampling of these is described as based on the adolescents' political commitment, the use of the Internet in this context and participants being between 16 and 25 years old (Picot and Willert, 2002, p. 226).

Here, the quantitative results provide the framework for the situation of adolescents in Germany at the time of the study, whereas the qualitative interviews provide insights into two specific areas – commitment and use of the Internet – which are deeper in two respects. First, for these areas in reference to the single cases that are portrayed. Second, the single cases have the function 'to present the views of the youth … The adolescents shall here become visible as the subjects of the interview' (p. 221).

Here again, both approaches have their own functions and both are put consistently into practice and used according to their particularities. The cross-references between both approaches and their results, however, remain rather limited. Instead, both results are presented complementarily and side by side.

QUALITATIVE AND INTERPRETIVE APPROACHES TO MIXED METHODS RESEARCH

For a long period, mixed methods research was seen as very strongly driven by quantitative ('positivistic') understandings of research – for example, Giddings (2006) criticized mixed methods research as 'positivism dressed in drag', as it mainly reduced the qualitative component of the mixed methods to a rather secondary role. This was a starting point for authors such as Hesse-Biber (2010a, 2010b), Morse (2010) or Hesse-Biber et al. (2015) and the editors of the 'other' handbook of mixed methods (Hesse-Biber and Johnson, 2015) to discuss a qualitatively driven mixed methods research. This discussion has two aims. First of all, to give qualitative approaches (or parts) in mixed methods discussions, research and practice more room and a stronger role. Second, to make the use of mixed methods more interesting in the context of originally qualitative projects or in qualitative research in general. Hesse-Biber (2010a, p. 457) raised two questions that are instructive for this discussion:

- How does the mixed methods design further the goals of a qualitative approach to understanding social reality?
- Why and how do qualitative researchers employ mixed methods research?

However, this discussion sticks to the more general focus of mixed methods research – discussions on mixed methods designs – but approaches it from the opposite direction. For this purpose, Hesse-Biber et al. (2015, pp. 6–9) have listed and briefly discussed a list of reasons why a qualitatively driven mixed methods design should be selected. They range from motives like generalization, to enhancing validity and reliability of qualitative findings, purposive use of quantitative findings and 'insight into the multiple layers of the experience of a phenomenon'.

These reasons can be summarized as follows. Some of them are strongly rooted in a quantitative concept of research, such as, for example, to test a theory developed from a qualitative study in a quantitative approach. Others suggest extending the qualitative part of a mixed methods study by adding a second qualitative substudy to develop a broader or fuller understanding of the issue that has been studied so far. The rest are intended to adapt the project more closely to the conditions in the field or to make the research more useful. The discussion, again, remains rather abstract in juxtaposing 'the' qualitative approach and 'the' quantitative approach. In her book, Hesse-Biber (2010c, Chapter 4) even goes one step further in discussing interpretative approaches to mixed methods research, aiming at understanding how people make sense of their social worlds, for which 'multiple views of social reality' should be studied (2010c, p. 104). Seeing this as distinct from qualitative research and not necessarily tied to qualitative methods, Hesse-Biber continues with case studies before discussing why an interpretative approach to research might use mixed methods. Here we find a shorter list of the reasons mentioned before for using a qualitatively driven mixed methods approach. Again there is less a detailed discussion of specific interpretative methods to be used in mixed methods research but more a general treatment of design issues similar to what was discussed before for qualitative approaches to mixed methods.

These two extensions of the mainstream discussions in mixed methods research methodology turn the focus around – from questions of how to integrate qualitative research into mixed methods research designs (as in the writings of authors such as Creswell and Plano Clark, 2011), to emphasizing the idea of how to use mixed methods research for and in the context of qualitative research. However, the main lines of the mixed methods research discussions are still pursued in such extensions – that mixed methods research means combinations of qualitative with quantitative research (in which relation or weighing it may become concrete) and that the main thing to discuss is issues of how to use the design types developed in this area. The idea of using combinations of various qualitative methods, for example, is not a serious alternative in the context of mixed methods research. As this is not the only shortcoming in this discussion, we will take a more integrative perspective on the possible links between mixed methods research and triangulation in the next chapter.

KEY POINTS

- There are several suggestions for how to design the combination of qualitative and quantitative research in mixed methods.
- In these designs, methods and data are combined in various ways.
- It should carefully be reflected upon why and how these designs and the mix of methods are applied.

FURTHER READING

These sources discuss the combination of qualitative and quantitative research in a reflective way:

Bryman, A. (1992) 'Quantitative and qualitative research: further reflections on their integration', in J. Brannen (ed.), *Mixing Methods: Quantitative and Qualitative Research*. Aldershot: Avebury, pp. 57–80.

Creswell, J.W. and Plano Clark, V.L. (2011) *Designing and Conducting Mixed Methods Research*. Thousand Oaks, CA: Sage.

Flick, U. (2014) *An Introduction to Qualitative Research*, 5th ed. London: Sage, Chapter 3.

Kelle, U. and Erzberger, C. (2004) 'Quantitative and qualitative methods: no confrontation', in U. Flick, E. von Kardorff and I. Steinke (eds), *A Companion to Qualitative Research*. London: Sage, pp. 172–7.

CHAPTER SEVEN

TRIANGULATION AS A FRAMEWORK FOR USING MIXED METHODS

CONTENTS

CHAPTER OBJECTIVES

After reading this chapter, you should know:

- which shortcomings in mixed methods research might prompt linking this approach with triangulation again;
- what characterizes an integrative perspective on triangulation and mixed methods;
- how triangulation can provide a framework for doing mixed methods research; and
- from an example, how this works.

TRIANGULATION AND MIXED METHODS IN QUALITATIVE RESEARCH

In the preceding chapters I have discussed the two major approaches to linking various methods (or approaches) in one study – triangulation and mixed methods – somewhat separately. Triangulation was discussed in terms of its background and methodological concepts of using it within or between methods in qualitative research and in ethnography as a research strategy. The focus was on the triangulation of qualitative methods. The combination of qualitative and quantitative approaches was unfolded in the context of mixed methods as the currently dominant approach for this combination. In this chapter a more integrative perspective will be taken (again) in three respects. First, it should be mentioned that the combination of qualitative research with quantitative methods has been an issue for triangulation for a long time as well (see Jick, 1983, for example). Second, critical views on the state of the methodological discussion (but also of the research practice) give the impression that the mixed methods discourse has some problematic areas still unresolved – for which a look at the methodological debates and suggestions in the field of triangulation can be helpful. And third, this more integrative perspective might make the use of mixed methods more attractive to qualitative researchers where it could be helpful for concrete studies. To begin with, what is the relation between triangulation and mixed methods?

Staking out the territories of triangulation and mixed methods research

The first answer is to see triangulation and mixed methods research as rather distinct approaches with differing agendas. While mixed methods research concentrates on and is limited to combining qualitative and quantitative research, triangulation is much more focused and concentrates on combining various qualitative approaches where the issue under study makes it necessary. This means triangulation and mixed methods can be distinguished in their areas of use in a broader field of multiple methods research. This also means that the original scope of multiple methods research – to combine whatever methods are necessary or helpful for understanding a social phenomenon under study – would be restored instead of reducing the general idea to a specific combination of (qualitative and quantitative) approaches. Then triangulation and mixed methods are understood as complementary concepts covering together a full range of research approaches to be combined. The limitations of this first understanding are twofold. First, it would not take into account that the methodological reflection in both concepts is different. Mixed methods is a rather pragmatic combination of two kinds of methods each seen in the closed form of paradigms, ignoring theoretical, epistemological and methodological differences between qualitative and quantitative research or the existence of various approaches in each of these camps for pragmatic purposes – to make the mix of quantitative and qualitative research work. Triangulation (of methods) has – in most cases – been embedded in methodological and epistemological reflections about what is combined and not limited to combining methods. If we take the division of labour model outlined above as a status quo for multiple methods discussion and practice, this means that qualitative and quantitative research will be combined on that rather pragmatist level, and that methodologically sound combinations are restricted to the field of qualitative research. It would also mean that the idea of triangulation including qualitative and quantitative approaches is abandoned and this field is left to mixed methods approaches.

Triangulation as a framework for integrating mixed methods

The second answer is to outline triangulation as a framework for integrating mixed methods, too, in a wider understanding of which approaches can be combined in social research. By introducing the triangulation of perspectives as a framework, we can make the mixed methods discussion a bit more methodologically reflected and sound again.

SOME PROBLEMATIC AREAS OF MIXED METHODS RESEARCH

Mixed methods research has been a booming field of methodological and theoretical discussion over the years. The boom has manifested in the publication of several journals (such as the *Journal of Mixed Methods Research*), three handbooks so far, a growing number of publications in special issues, edited books and textbooks and also single papers in journals concentrating on qualitative research (*Qualitative Inquiry*, *Qualitative Research*, etc.). In particular, this boom has led to expectations and requirements on the part of funding agencies that research in many fields should include a combination of quantitative and qualitative methods, and a readiness to prefer such projects and **proposal**s. But there are researchers – and among them more and more mixed methods research protagonists – who take such developments as a starting point for critically reflecting on this boom and the developments it has brought in a broader way. Perhaps these critical reflections, and in particular who they are coming from, can be seen as a slowly but continuously intensifying disenchantment with mixed methods research. In particular, issues of such reflections focus on questions such as: What were the developments in similar directions before the boom in mixed methods research, and what could be the contribution of the discussion about triangulation to the broader field of using multiple approaches in research? How far does the current discussion about mixed methods research take a rather narrow perspective on this field? What is (still) lacking in this discussion? What are the limitations that have developed in it concerning conceptualization, methodology, planning and doing mixed methods? And, how could an integrative perspective on mixed methods research advance the discussion including that on mixed methods research? Integration here is not so much focused on the integration of qualitative and quantitative research or methods (Morgan, 2014), but the integration of mixed methods and triangulation into a more comprehensive and more adequate concept of using multiple approaches in social research. Such questions will be discussed in this chapter.

A-historic views on mixed methods research

One problem in the discussion about mixed methods research is that it tries to give the impression that the whole approach and idea is something completely new. In his outline of 'an understanding of the basic characteristics of mixed methods research', Creswell (2015) holds: 'As a field of *methodology* about 25 years old, this approach has common elements that can easily be identified' (p. 1); other examples could also be mentioned. Against such an a-historic view, Maxwell (2016, p.12) argues that textbooks and methodological publications ignore the variety of the existing current research and in history before the label appeared. Historic antecedents have been discussed in Chapter 1. What is also more or less ignored in the methodological discourse about mixed methods research is the rather extended discussion about triangulation going back to Campbell and Fiske (1959) and Webb et al. (1966), further developed by Denzin (1970, 1989) and Flick (1992), that also includes the triangulation of qualitative and quantitative research (see Kelle and Erzberger, 2004). This discussion was the topic of Chapters 2–4 in this book. The current disenchantment (see Flick, 2017) about what has developed as mixed methods among some of the major protagonists made Sandelowski (2014), for example, engage in 'unmixing mixed-methods research' and suggest that 'mixed-methods research is better understood less as a new mode of inquiry than as a discursive re-packaging of the combinations' of theories, methodologies and the like 'constituting any empirical study' (2014, p. 3)

Sandelowski is not the only one to be sceptical (see below), so it might be useful to re-think some of the strengths and weaknesses of this approach in the next step.

Open questions in the methodology

In an editorial for the *Journal of Mixed Methods Research*, Greene (2008) has reviewed the development of the field and identified a number of open questions. The dimension of the characteristics of mixed methods has been neglected in the field's development (see p.17). She sees that little conceptual work on how to choose particular methods for a given inquiry purpose has been provided. The central question is still not sufficiently addressed: 'Around what does the mixing happen?'. And finally, it is unclear to her: 'What should a methodology of mixed methods research look like?' (Greene, 2008, p. 17). From this review, we may conclude that the methodological basis of mixed methods research is still rather underdeveloped and that there is little clarity about which methods are or should be combined for which purpose.

Issues or methods – methods or issues?

We do not find much about issues of research or specific forms of data, which orient the general stream of discussion. Instead, methods have come to the foreground of the whole discourse about mixed approaches in research.

Creswell (2009) has mapped the territory of *mixed methods research*. He compared it with the discussions at the mixed methods research conference in Cambridge 2008. His conclusion was that there was a general lack of papers dealing with theoretical issues, validity or defining mixed methods.

Research questions or universal research programme?

Bryman (2007) has done a study about the role of the research question in mixed methods research. He was interested in whether the assumption behind dealing with this issue in many textbooks – that designs, methods, and the like should be selected according to the issue under study – corresponded with the research practice of his interviewees. He interviewed 20 social scientists about their practices in and views about using combinations of quantitative and qualitative approaches – are they used because the issue under study requires it? He found two discourses. The first is 'a *particularistic* discourse' – that mixed methods should only be applied when this is appropriate to the particular research question of a study. This discourse basically confirms textbook views and suggests that a specific approach – such as mixed methods – should only be selected if there is a strong demand by the research question. The second discourse Bryman (2007) identified, 'a *universalistic* discourse', stresses that using mixed methods will lead to better results in any study, independent of the concrete aims and research questions of the study (2007, p. 8). This study and its results show how far an originally issues-specific approach – to use combinations of qualitative and quantitative research where the issue under study asks for it – has become more a discourse in itself, where the impression of mixed methods research as a better approach per se determines the planning of research. Plano Clark and Badiee (2010) in their chapter on research questions in mixed methods research do not refer to Bryman's study but discuss a similar distinction: 'Research questions dictate methods and research questions are the hub of the research process' (2010, p. 278). In their first alternative, the logic of the decisions seems closer to what Bryman discusses as 'particularistic' discourse, that there are specific research questions for legitimizing an approach while others (maybe most) are asking for a different one. But Plano Clark and Badiee then discuss mainly how research questions should be designed in mixed methods research, if there are any typologies of research questions in mixed methods and what influences such research questions. While this discussion may be helpful for clarifying the research questions pursued in a mixed methods study, it does not really focus on research questions as a framework for the decision on whether or not to use mixed methods and when. Again, this decision is rather assumed as made from the outset and then the issues around 'What is a good research question?' are reduced to a more technical problem.

If we extend Bryman's view with more recent reflections about this issue by Hesse-Biber (2015, p. 780), for example, – who holds that 'the framing of just what was mixed appears to have shifted to a more "universalist discourse" (Bryman, 2007) wherein "a priori" mixed methods risked being framed as "superior" to any mono-method' – the issue of using mixed methods where appropriate, or seeing it as a method for all, means becomes a more general problem in mixed methods.

Designs or issues as points of reference?

Hesse-Biber (2015) and Guest (2013) mention another problematic development in this context. They worry about the trend to set up typologies of designs for mixed methods research, which suggest that researchers only have to decide which of these designs they should apply to their study without asking any longer whether a mixed methods approach fits at all (or not) to what they want to study. This trend comes along with an 'unexamined belief in the "synergy" of mixed methods that suggests "two methods are better than one" ... and the growing popularity of a pragmatic "what works" approach as the "philosophical partner" to mixed methods' (Hesse-Biber, 2015, p. 776).

Limited range in the mix of methods

Bryman (2006a) has analyzed 232 articles published between 1994 and 2003 in which combinations of qualitative and quantitative methods were used. His criterion for selecting the papers was that the authors used the following keywords for their publications: 'qualitative and quantitative'; 'multi-method'; 'mixed method', 'triangulation'. Bryman found that the following methods were used in these studies: in 82.4% of the articles 'survey' (questionnaire, structured interview) was applied as a quantitative method; 71.1% of the articles referred to using (open, semi-structured) interviews as a qualitative method; 62.9% of the studies were based on cross-sectional designs both in the qualitative and in the quantitative part; 41.8% of the works were characterized by the combination of survey, interview and cross-sectional designs in both parts. From this analysis, we may conclude with Bryman, that the range of social science research methodology is exhausted and used in the context of mixed methods research in a rather limited way. And finally, combining interviews and questionnaires remains confined to a very similar and rather narrow range of data on both sides of the so-called 'qualitative–quantitative divide' in mixed methods research (see Sandelowski, 2014, for this point as well). This kind of reductionist approach to what is and should be 'mixed' as methods becomes evident also in the recent definition by Creswell (2015, p. 2), seeing mixed methods research as an approach combining 'quantitative (closed-ended) and qualitative (open-ended) data'. Qualitative interviews may be open-ended because they include open-ended questions, but if we have a look at other also very prominent forms of qualitative research, such as ethnography, the term 'open-ended' misses the point.

Only qualitative and quantitative methods to be combined?

Another point again becomes more and more questionable. If combinations of methods are necessary for an issue under study and if this is the starting point for deciding to use mixed methods, for example, why is there such a strong emphasis on just one form of combinations? In his recent book, Creswell (2015) gives a clear definition of what mixed methods is and what it is not (see Chapter 1 in this book). Similar restrictions can be found in the mission statement of the *Journal of Mixed Methods Research*, for example. In combination with the beliefs produced in the mixed methods discourse and discussed by Hesse-Biber (2015 – see above) – that mixed methods research per se is more valuable than other forms of research – this limited focus may reduce the range of social science research seen as valuable research in general.

The notion of paradigms

The interest in mixed methods research developed from the so-called 'paradigm wars' in the 1980s between qualitative and quantitative (or constructivist and positivist) research and the need to terminate that kind of debate and to return to more practical issues of research. Maybe this is the reason why the debate about mixed methods was so strongly linked to the notion of paradigms of qualitative and quantitative research. Stronger statements can be found in Johnson et al. (2007, p. 124), or in Morgan (2007) as well as in Greene (2007). However, there are a number of problems linked to the concept of 'paradigms' in this context. The first is, that Kuhn (1962) introduced this concept for describing: (1) how a specific science defined their issues, worldviews and methods, (2) to show how specific sciences defined themselves with their (dominant) paradigm, (3) to show that scientific progress does not proceed step-by-step but in revolutions, in which one paradigm is pushed aside by a new paradigm. That new paradigms develop and exist side by side is not so much the idea behind this concept. Despite all the rhetoric about first, second and (mixed methods research as) third movements, such a revolution has not happened, but we see quantitative, qualitative and mixed methods research existing in parallel.

The second – and maybe more important – problem is that this idea of the qualitative paradigm and (or vs.) the quantitative paradigm (or the Qual and Quan symbolizations) gives the impression that there is one type of qualitative research, for example, which can be described and defined by the same features, goals, methods, and the like. Looking into the history of qualitative research or into journals such as *Qualitative Inquiry* gives a different impression. Debates about the globalization of qualitative research (Flick, 2014b), or overviews of qualitative research in Europe (Knoblauch et al., 2005) or in Germany and the USA (Flick, 2005), show more differentiation than could be unified by a paradigm of qualitative research. And in the quantitative part of mixed methods, we will find a similar situation. Morgan (2007) has argued 'for a version of paradigms as systems of beliefs and practices that influence how researchers select both the questions they study and methods that they use to study them' (2007, p.49). But again, in the rhetoric of combination in mixed methods research, we have the rather closed notion of a qualitative and a quantitative paradigm.

A third problem is mentioned by Symonds and Gorard (2010). They underline that the use of the 'paradigm' concept in mixed methods research intensifies the juxtaposition of qualitative *vs.* quantitative research rather than bringing the opposites together. They see two effects. First, that researchers now simply choose between the two 'paradigms' – or the three if mixed methods research as a third one is included – instead of planning and designing their research according to the needs of their study. Second, the notion of these 'paradigms' transmitted in the literature and in teaching obscures the common features of the diverse approaches in social research – needs for planning, combinations of interpretation and sometimes counting in qualitative approaches, and of counting and interpretations in quantitative research, etc. (see Flick, 2015, for a comparative outline of qualitative and quantitative research).

From method to method – the narrative behind the three handbooks of mixed methods research

One feature of the methodological discussion and publications about mixed methods research has always been a strong orientation on methods – to be used and to be mixed. This orientation on methods is also visible in the basic structure of Tashakkori and Teddlie's handbook (2003a). Here the central part (Part II) is about methods issues – like design, control, analysis and display – which is framed by two other parts. The first part is about background theories and the history of mixed methods research and the third part gives a survey of fields of application of mixed methods research.

Not mentioned as a prominent issue for the discussion, first, are specific issues of research, which ask for using mixed methods research. This would help researchers in deciding when and why to use mixed methods research approaches for their own issues of study – and when it would be better to refrain from this strategy. Neither mentioned, as a prominent issue for discussion, are data or combinations of data in mixed methods research. What does it mean for the research practice to have a specific diversity in different forms or sets of data? What are the implications of different forms of data for analyzing them? All this is more and more subordinated to the claim of a general strategy of mixed methods research, which is ready to replace other forms of research. This has also to do with the claim that we have a third movement of research (mixed methods research) now, which is ready to replace earlier movements (quantitative as the first and qualitative as the second movement of research – Tashakkori and Teddlie, 2003a). This is embedded in the far-reaching claims that are made for combinations of qualitative and quantitative research in general, which could raise the expectation that the strongly differentiated range of methods in both areas should be used and combined in mixed methods research.

Although the second edition of this handbook (Tashakkori and Teddlie, 2010) comes with quite a number of new chapters (or chapters written by different authors) the basic structure and focus remain the same. The major difference and step forward is that Part I now discusses a number of theoretical frameworks for using mixed methods research (feminism, transformative purposes) or concepts as a basis for using these frameworks (pragmatism, realism, dialectics) and includes a number of self-reflexive chapters (interviews with protagonists). However, what is still missing are: (1) considerations about the (theoretical and epistemological) differences in the various methods to combine, and how to take these into account in the research practice of mixing methods; and (2) there is still not much about for what purposes (research questions and issues) and why mixed methods research should be used – the methodological discussions always start after the decision to use mixed methods research has already been taken.

The third handbook (Hesse-Biber and Johnson, 2015) takes a broader approach than the other ones in two respects. First, there is considerable attention paid to integrating the earlier approach of multi-method research (Hunter and Brewer, 2006) and to setting up a merger between the two approaches (or warning against such a merger – Greene, 2015). Interestingly enough, the multi-method approach (and its creators) are given the stage in a chapter on 'Designing multimethod research' (Hunter and Brewer, 2015) or integrated in more general mixed methods research chapters. Second, a strong emphasis is laid on a qualitatively driven approach to mixed methods research in the handbook (e.g. in Hesse-Biber et al., 2015). This discussion has been going on for some time, which is on the one hand a step forward, as more room and interest is given to qualitative research in mixed methods research. On the other hand, the need for this discussion demonstrates that mixed methods research in its first decades was dominantly informed by quantitative research and thinking. But in the end, this newer discussion again starts with methods (now qualitative) for a methodological discussion, in which the use of mixed methods research is not really questioned in terms of when and why but a starting point set before any methodological discussion. That does not mean that the chapters in this or the earlier handbooks are not good or not helpful for doing mixed methods research. But they again in general tie down methodological discussion and reflection to technical details (how to design or sample, what are examples of mixed methods in various fields of application, how is it done there? and the like).

From simple pragmatics to pragmatism – the theory problem of mixed methods research

The fascination of mixed methods research in part results from the exhaustive debates about qualitative vs. quantitative research in the 1980s (the so-called paradigm wars) and the underlying debate about what is research, what is good research and what is not. Interestingly enough, important impulses for developing mixed methods research came from evaluation research (Greene, 2007; Greene and Caracelli, 1997), where some kind of 'what works' attitude was and still is not uncommon. Methods are often selected or combined without investing too much time into fundamentalist discussions. In this context, Greene (2007), for example, quotes with some emphasis (see p. 50) Miles and Huberman (1984): 'Epistemological purity doesn't get research done' (1984, p. 21). A criticism against mixed methods research was quite often that a too pragmatic use (and combination) of methods, without thinking much about their underlying assumptions (and differences) has been practised (e.g. Denzin, 2010). The reaction in the methodological literature of mixed methods research was to look for theoretical foundations that could epistemologically justify the continuation of a rather pragmatic research practice. The first candidate here is a new reading of pragmatism (e.g. Morgan, 2007) or to look for other overarching frameworks (e.g. feminism and how mixed methods research is used and justified in this context, e.g. Hesse-Biber, 2010a). These strategies of re-theorizing mixed methods research may or may not work, but the theory problem of mixed methods research is on a different level. The combinations are and remain methods-centred and neglect internal theoretical differences in conceptualizing research and issues. On the one hand between qualitative and quantitative approaches, but on the other hand between various qualitative approaches and also between various quantitative approaches.

Such differences are not just biases or the like, but lead to differences in how issues under study are conceptualized, what is seen as relevant and what kind of methodological approach is necessary. At this point, methodology comes into the game – which means the relation of issue–theory–method. Then the question is: 'How can mixed methods take the methodological underpinnings and frameworks of the methods that are combined into account?'. 'How can mixed methods deal with conflicting or varying methodologies in a design?' is the question rather than 'What is a methodology of mixed methods research?' (similar to Greene, 2008).

TRIANGULATION AS A FRAMEWORK FOR MIXED METHODS RESEARCH

Systematic triangulation of perspectives

In Chapter 2, we outlined the 'systematic triangulation of perspectives': different research perspectives are triangulated in order to complement their strengths and to show their limits. The aim is not a pragmatic combination of different methods, but to take into account their theoretical backgrounds. Different perspectives can become concrete in analyzing knowledge (with interviews) and practices (with conversation analysis or observations), but also in analyzing subjective experiences of an illness (in interviews) and frequencies and distributions of that illness in the population (with epidemiological and statistical methods). The aim of such a triangulation is less to confirm results but rather to include complementary (subjective experiences complementing the prevalence of an illness) or contradictory results (knowledge about vs. practices concerning health risks). A systematic triangulation of perspectives can be realized with several qualitative but also with qualitative and quantitative methods. It becomes systematic, once not only methods are combined but also when their theoretical and epistemological backgrounds are taken into account in the combination.

If we start from the concept of *comprehensive triangulation*, also outlined in Chapter 2, and use it as a framework for doing mixed methods research more reflectively, we can proceed as follows and establish links to some parts of the discussion about mixed methods research.

Investigator triangulation as a collaborative strategy

In a *comprehensive triangulation*, investigator triangulation would be the first step. Collaboration of several researchers with differing theoretical, epistemological and methodological backgrounds can be a relevant part of mixed methods research in two respects: either a source of conflict (between and about these backgrounds) or a source for a productive division of labour. Archibald (2015) has recently discussed integrating the concept of investigator triangulation in mixed methods research practice, and highlighted its relevance on the basis of a critical review of the mixed methods research literature (journal articles and textbooks). She concludes that this strategy has been widely ignored in mixed methods research, but could be used for exploring the tensions on paradigmatic and methodological levels and to develop models of collaboration in mixed methods research practice.

In our research on residents' sleeping problems in nursing homes (see Flick et al., 2012), we started from a collaboration of researchers with two kinds of backgrounds – epidemiologists and statisticians on the one hand and qualitative researchers on the other. We had several professional groups in the team (psychology, nursing, medicine and sociology), which allowed investigator triangulation on several levels.

Theory triangulation conceived as triangulation of theoretical perspectives

Investigator triangulation in this sense offers a different potential for using theory triangulation in the context of mixed methods research. Investigators with differing methodological and professional backgrounds bring several theoretical perspectives into the collaboration. These differing theoretical perspectives may become concrete in the methods selected for understanding the issue under study. If they do not just remain implicit as some kind of tacit knowledge (Polanyi, 1966) about how to do research, but are made explicit and openly discussed they allow us to take several theoretical, methodological and methods-theoretical perspectives on the issue of the study. In the example of our study, sleeping problems in nursing homes can be seen either as a problem of incidence (how often do they occur?), coincidence (correlating with which other health problems), consequences (participation in social activities in the institution) or treatment (how often are sleeping pills prescribed for treating them?). This perspective asks for frequencies, correlations and the like. Or they can be understood as an issue of professional awareness (what are representations of the issue held by nurses or doctors?), reflected practices (how are sleeping problems taken into account in nursing practices or in medical practices beyond medications?) and improvement of such practices (which knowledge and awareness is necessary and how can this be improved?). The triangulation of these perspectives on a theoretical and methodological level provides a theoretical ground for combining the qualitative and quantitative (or several qualitative) methods needed for approaching the problem from several angles.

Methodological triangulation

If we take that outline of perspectives on an issue seriously, the limitations of possible methods to be combined (triangulated or mixed) should be linked to the issue under study and not to a 'paradigm' and *a priori* settings. Methodological triangulation is not just the combination of methods. It is rather the triangulation of methodologies including methods and their theoretical, epistemological and conceptual backgrounds. Finally the starting point is less a specific combination of methods (if at all), but which method(s) the issue under study requires for being understood in the research.

Data triangulation

The triangulation of several forms of data is then the result from the option of triangulating various methods. The challenge here is not to replace data triangulation by mixed methods designs as Tashakkori and Teddlie (2003b) suggest, but how to integrate the various perspectives in the data generated for understanding the issue of research. In our example, we had routine data about assessments and prescriptions linked to sleeping problems and several kinds of interview data about treatment practices and problem awareness in professional groups. The challenges were how to link these data and how to find levels of abstraction for making such links meaningful. Using the term 'triangulation' in this context, Erzberger and Kelle (2003) discuss a number of issues and strategies of inferences – between qualitative and quantitative methods/data but also between the levels of method and data on the one hand and theories on the other hand.

Systematic triangulation of perspectives instead of mixing paradigms

Finally, the concept of a systematic triangulation of perspectives can offer a way out of the problems linked to using the paradigm concept (see above) in mixed methods research. Systematic triangulation of perspectives (see Flick, 1992, p. 183) means to combine research perspectives (theory/methodology/methods) when studying an issue.

At the same time, the term 'perspectives' refers to different ways of addressing a phenomenon – for example, the (subjective) perspective of an individual who is concerned with the issue in the role of a patient, or the (subjective) perspective of an individual who is dealing with this issue as a professional. 'Perspective' can also mean the institutional routines through which this issue or the treatment of the health-related issue (how often it occurs, how often it is documented in the form of a diagnosis, etc.) is documented. 'Perspective' finally refers to methods that are closely embedded in the theoretical–methodological background of including mixed methods where they are useful.

If these perspectives are to be unfolded from different angles, e.g. professional and lay knowledge, and on different levels, such as knowledge, practices and routines, a variety of methods and data are needed. If the diversity of these perspectives is taken seriously, a systematic triangulation of perspectives can provide a methodological framework concerning the links between the research subject, theory, methods and data for using mixed methods in a methodologically more elaborated way.

EXAMPLE: RESIDENTS' SLEEP DISORDERS IN NURSING HOMES

In our study on sleep disorders and their management in long-term care facilities that is presented here as an example, we selected an 'embedded design' (in accordance with Creswell and Plano Clark, 2011). We started by looking at the prevalence of sleep disorders in an institutionalized German population suffering from multiple diseases. At the same time, we wanted to answer the question of the extent to which sleep disorders represent a threat to the functional status and the remaining health of nursing home residents. Both questions are quantitative in nature, and consequently, we chose quantitative methods with which to answer them. However, from a constructivist approach, we wanted to understand staff awareness and knowledge of sleep problems. Under what circumstances do staff members actively treat the sleep disorders of their clients, and when do they neglect these problems? Are professional knowledge and competence or rather the residents' status or wishes the decisive determinants of ways of dealing with the problem? Are members of staff aware that sleep disorders are serious health problems? These questions required the application of methods that would reach under the surface of the socially accepted explanations. Moreover, we wanted to explore staff concepts of intervention, including their professional and common-sense prejudices. The episodic interview (Flick, 2000a) seemed to be the most appropriate methodological approach. In addition, we wanted to learn more about the residents of nursing homes and their beliefs, taking into account the necessity of treatment for their sleep problems. These are issues that have not previously been analyzed, and therefore, a qualitative method was considered to be suitable for the first exploration (Flick, 2011). Finally, we wanted to see the extent to which drugs – hypnotics and psychoactive medication – were actually given to the residents of nursing homes, and what else was done for those who suffered from serious sleep disturbances. Here, the appropriate basis for the analysis contained quantitative data from the standardized assessment and data on medical prescriptions.

Thus, different perspectives were triangulated systematically in our study and, correspondingly, mixed methods were also used for the collection and analysis of the data. This is an example of systematic triangulation of the kind that is required if the subject of the study is a very complex phenomenon, like sleep disorders in institutional settings. Our first question, which related to their prevalence and distribution, is epidemiological in nature, and, therefore, the use of a quantitative epidemiological approach was deemed appropriate. The functional and general health-related consequences of disturbed sleep should be measured using health indicators. The basis for this measurement was a standardized and fully structured assessment that contained a variety of valid and reliable scales. In practice, the Minimum Data Set of the Resident Assessment Instrument 2.0 was used (Morris et al., 1995), which contains up to 320 variables: cognitive status, mood, behaviour, communication, social relations, activities of daily living, occupation, health problems, diagnoses, as well as data on medical treatment, different therapies and programmes. Thus, a comprehensive picture of three samples of nursing home residents in Berlin, Germany (total $n = 7,505$) was available. For the measurement of sleep disturbances, variables on the difficulty of falling asleep and staying asleep, non-restful sleep, and a disturbed wake–sleep cycle were used. Longitudinal data were obtained on 1,375 residents who stayed and/ or survived for more than three years in long-term care facilities.

To study the professional constructions of managing sleep disorders with regard to residents suffering from sleep disturbances, and in particular awareness of this problem, the motivation to act, and efforts actually made by nurses and physicians (see Flick et al., 2010), a methodological procedure with an in-depth orientation was required. The same was the case for the relatively unknown phenomenon of residents' views of their own disturbed sleep and the therapy that they received. The real situation (the amount of drugs supplied, the frequency and duration of treatment by therapists, and the adequacy of treatment) was measured on the basis of prescription data and by information incorporated into the assessment.

The data that formed the basis for the analysis of the professionals' perspective were supplied by episodic interviews with physicians ($n = 20$) and nurses ($n = 32$). The episodic interviews addressed two different forms of 'knowledge': semantic knowledge based on concepts and their relations (What are sleep disorders? What factors influence sleep?) and episodic knowledge based on memories of situations (e.g. a situation in which the doctor treated sleep problems with medication). The interviewees were asked to report on interventions that they normally used against sleeping problems. The interviews focused on the interviewees' knowledge, understanding, and awareness of the sleep disorders of residents in nursing homes. One issue addressed in the interviews was the treatment of sleep disorders using drugs. The following questions were asked: 'According to your experience, how important is the use of drugs for the treatment of sleep disorders?'; 'Could you describe situations in which you would decide to prescribe medication for sleep disorders?'; and 'What advantages and disadvantages do sleeping pills have for your target group, according to your experience?'.

Four groups of nurses were interviewed: geriatric nurses, general nurses, nursing auxiliaries, and caregivers without a formal qualification. The issue of care for individuals suffering from sleep disorders was introduced in a case vignette referring to a very old resident with repeated sleep disorders and nurses who were discussing administering a sleeping pill. Questions relating to this vignette were as follows: 'What would you do in such a case?' and 'What would you use in such a situation?'. In the few cases in which the nurses did not refer spontaneously to medication, they were asked for their experiences with sleeping pills and about when they would support this treatment and what disadvantages they perceived (for more details about the interviews with the nurses, see Flick et al., 2010).

Benefits of using mixed methods in triangulation

In this study, we triangulated a number of perspectives on a phenomenon: interviews with different groups involved in the treatment of sleep disorders (doctors, nurses and residents), with the aim of analyzing attitudes toward the use of medication for this purpose. We applied this form of triangulation in earlier studies, in which we studied doctors' and nurses' concepts of health and ageing using interviews and focus groups (Flick et al., 2003) and clients' and service providers' views on service utilization in the context of chronic illness and homelessness (Flick, 2010). These studies did not include data about the frequency of health problems or documenting health care practices. We tried to fill this gap in the new study. To understand the extent to which the attitudes that became visible in the interviews in this study corresponded with treatment practices and the relevance of sleep disorders, we used a mixed methods approach, adding an epidemiological analysis (focusing on the prevalence of sleep problems and the relative frequencies of drug treatment) to a social-science-based study.

TRIANGULATION: TOWARD A MORE SYSTEMATIC USE OF MIXED METHODS

If we return to the more general discussion about triangulation and mixed methods, we may first re-address the starting point for the use of mixed methods. Our research started from a field (nursing homes), a problem (sleep disorders), and the complexity of the problem in the field, which led to the selection of a number of methods for studying this complex phenomenon. To conceptualize and run the study, we needed researchers with different backgrounds – epidemiologists and qualitative researchers for investigator triangulation as discussed above. The disciplinary perspectives they brought to the study allowed us to realize a theoretical triangulation. To understand this complexity on a methodological level, we needed first a quantitative approach that revealed the relevance and frequency of this problem. Then, we needed qualitative approaches to understand the experiences and attitudes of the people suffering from this problem and the awareness and practices of those dealing with this problem as professionals. Finally, quantitative approaches provided information about how the reported attitudes diverged from the documented prescription practices. The triangulation of these methods included a mixed methods approach and produced a variety of data, in the sense of data triangulation.

This example may illustrate why and how particular methods are selected for a specific project – one of the open questions that Greene (2008) mentions regarding mixed methods research. The combination of methods is based on specific perspectives – what are the institutional and subjective representations of the issue and its treatment? This may answer the second question Greene raises regarding mixed methods: around what does the mixing happen? A methodology (which Greene sees as something to be further developed for mixed methods research) of the systematic triangulation of perspectives could be devised based on the idea that data on different levels should be produced. In our example, we achieved this by integrating several perspectives on an issue – the views of professionals and residents – and data on several levels (representations and practices). This methodology should also include a plan of the research and of any combination of approaches that goes beyond the combination of methods per se, and refers to the linking of different theoretical perspectives and, perhaps, researchers with different backgrounds (both of which are suggested by Denzin, 1970).

Rather than seeking confirmation of findings, we should combine approaches that allow mosaics to be created out of research issues. All this can be relevant for testing the limits of research methods and crossing their boundaries within qualitative research. However, it can also be necessary and relevant to go beyond that area and to advance to a more comprehensive approach to integrated research, including mixed methods, as in the example presented above. In such a study, the theoretical perspectives on vulnerability, for example, can be addressed. If these perspectives are to be unfolded from different angles (professional and lay knowledge) and on different levels (knowledge, practices and routines), a variety of methods and data are needed. If the diversity of these perspectives is taken seriously, a systematic triangulation of perspectives can provide a methodological framework (concerning the links between the research subject, theory, methods and data) for using mixed methods.

KEY POINTS

- Mixed methods are confronted by some problematic areas on conceptual and practical levels.
- Triangulation has a stronger theoretical and methodological background.
- Triangulation can be used as a framework for using mixed methods in a more reflective way.

FURTHER READING

Triangulation

Triangulation and its theoretical basis are spelled out in more detail in the following sources:

Denzin, N.K. (1989) *The Research Act*, 3rd ed. Englewood Cliffs, NJ: Prentice-Hall.
Flick, U. (2018) 'Triangulation', in N.K. Denzin and Y.S. Lincoln (eds), *The SAGE Handbook of Qualitative Research*, 5th ed. London and Thousand Oaks, CA: Sage, pp. 444–61.

Mixed methods

Mixed methods and their theoretical basis are spelled out in more detail in the following sources:

Creswell, J.W. (2015) *A Concise Introduction to Mixed Methods Research*. Los Angeles, CA: Sage.
Flick, U. (2017) 'Mantras and myths: the disenchantment of mixed methods research and revisiting triangulation as a perspective', *Qualitative Inquiry*, 23 (1), 46–58.
Greene, J.C. (2007) *Mixed Methods in Social Inquiry*. San Francisco, CA: Jossey-Bass.

CHAPTER EIGHT

HOW TO USE TRIANGULATION AND MIXED METHODS IN QUALITATIVE RESEARCH

PRACTICAL ISSUES

CONTENTS

CHAPTER OBJECTIVES

After reading this chapter, you should know about:

- the practical problems of using triangulation and mixed methods in qualitative research;
- how to plan sampling and comparison in using triangulation and mixed methods; and
- where you can integrate triangulation and mixed methods in the research process.

In the preceding chapters, I have used several examples from studies in which triangulation or mixed methods were applied for advancing qualitative research at the level of combining different approaches and results. Then we looked at a number of examples of using mixed methods in qualitative studies. In what follows, some of the known practical problems from such applications will be reviewed again. This time the focus will be on how to plan and use triangulation and/or mixed methods in qualitative research.

DESIGN

Triangulation in case studies

For the design of a study using triangulation, similar questions arise as for designs in qualitative research in general (see Flick, 2018b). Triangulation can be used in the context of one of the basic designs in qualitative research. You can plan a case study using a variety of data sorts or different methods or theoretical approaches. Hildenbrand (1999) describes, for his approach to case reconstruction, how he studies families as cases and first produces protocols of observations, which are then complemented by conversations about the family history and the analysis of documents.

Mixed methods in case studies

In particular, if the case under study is not of an individual, but, for example, an institution, mixed methods can be used in case studies as well. Greene and Hall (2010, pp. 133–7) present a case study in which a specific school is studied using a sequential design (qualitative observations, questionnaire, in-depth interviews, overall interpretations and **member checks**) to analyze the school's capacity to make the school improvement work that is required by the US federal policy of 'No Child Left Behind' (p. 133).

Comparative studies

Studies using triangulation can also be planned as comparative studies. For the possible forms of comparisons, there are a multitude of options located at various levels. First, you can plan comparison across the cases at the level of the application of one method: what are the commonalities and differences in the knowledge of the various interviewees (case 1–N) or in the practices of different participants (case 1–N)? Furthermore, we can compare the results of comparisons across the cases from applying both methods: what are the commonalities and differences of knowledge in relation to those of practices? And finally, we can draw comparisons of the cases for the convergences and divergences at the level of the single case: can we elaborate a typology of relations between knowledge and practices? (See Table 8.1.)

TABLE 8.1 Dimensions of comparison in studies using triangulation

Method I		Method II
$case_1$	Comparison	$case_1$
$case_2$	Comparison	$case_2$
...		...
$case_N$	Comparison	$case_N$
Comparison $case_{1-N}$	Comparison	Comparison $case_{1-N}$
	Comparison	

In mixed methods studies the comparison in Table 8.1 can be applied in a similar way if the participants in the qualitative part of the study are also included in the quantitative study and can be identified in its sample. If not, the comparisons will focus on what the comparisons in each method have revealed and compare that. For example, all interviews are compared and a typology has been developed that is compared to the trends resulting from comparing all the participants in the questionnaire study.

Temporal sequencing

As was already mentioned for the mix of qualitative and quantitative methods, different forms of triangulation can be used for (only) qualitative methods, but three alternatives can be planned in temporal respects. Several qualitative methods can be used in parallel: at the same time as observation, interviews are done or the interviewee is immediately asked to provide a consultation. Different methods can be used in sequence: first all interviews are done and then a period of observation follows (or recordings of consultations are collected) or vice versa. Finally, the methods can be applied in an interlaced way: first observation, then interviews, then observation again. Both strings of research can be referred to one another. That can be applied to mixed methods research in a similar way. Here, the types of design suggested by Creswell and Plano Clark (2011) can be a helpful orientation – for mixed methods and for triangulation as well.

Cross-sectional and longitudinal studies

Most studies using triangulation are done as cross-sectional studies. The integrated panel design that Kluge (2001) has presented includes several waves of interviews and standardized surveys (see Chapter 6). This can be transferred to the combination of several qualitative methods. Then, people would be interviewed repeatedly during an extended period, or observations are carried out for a longer period and interviews are conducted in between phases of observations. Beyond that there are few longitudinal studies in qualitative research (Lüders, 2004b); the approach is extended in its range (more methods) and in time dimensions (repeated application of the methods) and the research design becomes over-complex compared to the usual qualitative research project. The same applies to mixed methods. Most research is based on cross-sectional designs (see Bryman, 2006a) but trends to extend mixed methods research to longitudinal studies are intensifying. For the qualitative leg in such studies, it should be taken into account how far interviews, for example, can be applied repeatedly to the same participants.

Planning of resources

In calculating the resources (time, methodological skills, costs, etc.) for a study using triangulation, you should take into account that researchers should have experience with the different methods, either in every method or in a division of labour. Because of the complexity of calculating the resources for organizing and running the research, much more is needed than what Miles and Huberman (1994, p. 47) or Morse (1998) suggest as resources for the single steps of qualitative research (see also Flick, 2018b). In the numerous textbooks on mixed methods research, not much attention is paid to the topic of resources. An exception is provided by Creswell and Plano Clark (2011, p. 13), who mention first the question of skills the researcher needs in both areas (qualitative and quantitative research) at least on a basic level. This parallels the discussion in Kelle (2001) who problematizes the potential (over-)

challenge for the individual researcher to be skilled in more than one method to use triangulation. Creswell and Plano Clark (2011, p. 14) also mention other resources to be reflected on, such as time for working with two kinds of data, resources for collecting both qualitative and quantitative data, and the necessary skills and staff available in the research team. Creswell and Plano Clark strongly recommend working in teams with several researchers and various skills, even if that increases the costs and may make collaboration a complicated process (2011, p. 15).

These suggestions again can be applied to using triangulation of several qualitative methods. Finally, we can transfer the question of the relation of the single methods from the discussion about linking qualitative and quantitative research. Are methods used on an equal footing or is one method placed over the other or subordinated – are there primary or secondary methods?

SAMPLING

From the research question, sampling strategies lead to concrete goals as to which empirical 'units' should be in involved in the study. The range goes from rather abstract (for example, according to a statistical numerical model) strategies like random sampling to more concrete strategies, which are based more on the contents of the study (like theoretical sampling according to Glaser and Strauss, 1967) or a variant of purposive sampling (according to Patton, 2015; see also Flick, 2014a, Chapter 13). Referring to sampling in studies using triangulation or mixed methods, we can discuss mainly three aspects. (1) How can we guarantee that a sampling strategy fitting each single method can also be put into practice in the context of triangulation or mixed methods? (2) Which options of an interlaced sampling make sense? (3) How can we take into account or bring together the different logical approaches of sampling of different methods?

One sampling strategy for different methods

In our study on concepts of health and ageing, a sample of doctors and nurses in two cities was constructed according to certain criteria (Flick et al., 2004, Chapter 3; Flick, 2018b) and used in practice. In the focus groups, which were run more than a year later, in principle the same sample should have been used. However, a number of dropouts occurred. Some interviewees said right away that they were not interested in participating in one of the groups. Others had to cancel shortly before the date of the group. In analyzing the results of the groups and even more in linking them to the interviews, such differences have to be taken into consideration.

Interlaced sampling

Interlaced sampling means that cases or groups for the application of the second method are selected from the sample drawn for the first method. For example, from a sample for a survey, some cases are selected that make up the sample for open interviews. Against the background of the interviews with several counsellors a sample is drawn from them (according to theoretical sampling). The members of this sample are asked to provide the recording of a consultation for conversation analysis to be applied – the second method in the triangulation. From observing an open space on a playing field, single cases are selected for interviews by using their social localization in the observed social fabric as the criterion. In all these examples, substantial criteria can be developed from one part of the study for selecting the cases for the second part (see the example on coping with cancer in Chapter 5).

Different logical approaches of sampling

Finally, in the application of different methods it should be considered whether they each call for different samples. For interviews, sampling will address people. In observations it is rather the situation that is the focus of sampling. Thus, it will not necessarily be the same persons who have to be included in the observation as were selected for the interviews. When questionnaires are used, participants are selected in a random sampling, whereas for interviews a purposive sampling is more adequate. In a quantitative sampling it is important to calculate sample size and representativity. In qualitative sampling, it is important to select the participants who can answer the questions you want to ask most informatively or who are most helpful for understanding what you are studying. Here it is often difficult to define in advance how many participants you should integrate or 'how many interviews are enough' (Baker and Edwards, 2012). Creswell (2015) spells out the issue of sampling for the designs he and his colleagues have identified as typical for mixed methods research. In the end the main problem to solve in concrete projects is that the sampling logic may be different for each method applied; samples in one study are different in their sizes, in their structure and are oriented on different ideas of representativeness.

SPECIAL PROBLEMS OF ACCESS

Sampling is the plan for what to integrate, field access makes it work (if successful), changes it (in case of problems) or makes it fail (if there is some kind of resistance in the field against the research or researchers). Wolff (2004) describes the problems that can arise when entering a field of investigation, and discusses what we can learn from them and the possible solutions. He makes clear that social research in general and qualitative research in particular come with impositions on the field under study and its members. Examples of such impositions are to make time available, let people in, face maybe embarrassing questions or issues, or accept a methodological regime (e.g. of certain types of question). Participants should also understand what researchers want from them, trust them, and answer questions for them which are maybe (no longer or not) relevant for themselves (Wolff, 2004, pp. 195–6).

In studies using several methods, this imposition of research is intensified even more. On the one hand, the impositions are doubled by the use of two (or more) methods. On the other hand, the time needed for participating in the study grows (not only is an interview to be given, but also continuous observation or the recording of conversations or filling in a questionnaire are to be accepted, etc.). This relatively higher effort increases the danger that potential participants turn down the researcher and are not available for the study. In my study on trust in counselling, I had to face the extra problem of a selective readiness: several of the counsellors whom I had approached according to theoretical sampling with good reasons, agreed to give an interview, but not to have a consultation with a client recorded for research purposes. Others had no problem with such a recording, but would not agree to an interview. Both can lead to a considerable loss of interesting or – in terms of sampling – relevant cases.

Another problem in this context is that in combining interviews with observations in open spaces (markets, train stations, etc.), it is sometimes not possible to include all the people who are frequenting these spaces systematically in the study and have them interviewed and observed, and to obtain some kind of **informed consent** about being studied from them. In the case of using mixed methods, participants have to adapt to two logical approaches of research – for example, to present very personal details and experience on the one hand and very limited and focused answers (ticking a box in answering a questionnaire question) on the other if they take part in both legs of the study.

COLLECTION AND INTERPRETATION OF DATA
Influences on the subject

In this respect, some of the points already mentioned above for design issues apply for studies with triangulation or mixed methods. You should at least take time effects into account. When the different (qualitative or quantitative) methods are applied one after the other, you should reflect on how to take into consideration the time between data collections with both methods. In our study on health and ageing concepts, more than a year elapsed between the (first) interviews and the focus groups. In the meantime, the issue to be mentioned in the interviews and focus groups may have changed considerably – in this case, for example, due to political discussions of health in the media, professional organizations, or in legal terms or political planning. Accordingly we should think about how far the participants in the interviews and later in the focus groups still talk about 'the same' and how to reflect those developments in the data and their interpretation. The same can become relevant for sequential designs as suggested for mixed methods.

Interferences between different methods

A second aspect is the interferences between the different methods of data collection. In mixing quantitative and qualitative methods – for example, questionnaires and interviews – the relatively strong structure in the research situation in the standardized questionnaire may produce or confirm specific expectations towards research, which may radiate into the second research situation, so that the more open flow in narratives or the interview dialogue may be influenced by expectations for more structure. This may have the consequence that it will be more difficult to effectively use the strengths of the interview – its open structure – than it would have been without using a standardized method before. Similar influences are possible the other way around.

We should think about how to deal with knowledge from the other data collection. What the researchers know about the participants' knowledge from the interviews may lead them to just look for confirmatory (or contradictory) practices or events in the observation. This becomes relevant if we want to use triangulation with the focus on assessing the quality of the interview data and analysis (or of one method with the other), but also with the focus on consequently exploiting the full epistemological potential of each method. The same effects may occur with the insights provided from questionnaire data influencing what is asked and further explored in the interviews and what is ignored.

Such interferences can be used purposively if researchers orient themselves in questions in an interview on what they learned from observations beforehand and focus directly on specific points in relation to them. Also, statements and results from interviews can be used to focus later observations more strongly. In a similar way, we deliberately used statements from the previous interviews to stimulate the discussion in the focus groups with doctors or nurses in our health and ageing project.

In both cases it is essential to deal with such interferences in a reflective way, which means to clarify how to use or perhaps avoid them and to do this for every single case in a comparable way.

Interpretation

In analyzing the different (kinds of) data coming up in a study using triangulation or mixed methods, the point just made for data collection can be further elaborated. Here, we can think of different strategies for linking the data. Each set of data can be analyzed separately. First, all interviews are compared in order to derive commonalities and tendencies. Then all observations are analyzed in a comparative way. Commonalities and tendencies are referred against the results from analyzing the interviews and vice versa.

Both kinds of data can also be referred against each other at the level of the single case and then analyzed. Finally, we can develop categories for the second set of data from analyzing the first one. From analyzing consultations, we can develop a general process model of consultation in the specific context under study. The phases of counselling that become evident here, come with specific 'tasks' for the counsellor in building a trustful relationship with the client. At the beginning of the conversation a relationship has to be established, a problem has to be identified, named and explored, and the clients have to be given enough space to unfold their views of their problems. From these tasks, we can derive categories for analyzing the subjective theories of the counsellors that have been reconstructed in previous interviews. These categories can be useful for showing how far such phases and tasks are represented in the counsellors' knowledge in reference to how to put them into practice or in an idealizing way.

For within-method triangulation, it may be useful to analyze the different sorts of data separately and in a contrasting way. For example, we can contrast the contents of narratives with those of subjective definitions. The question then is, for example, which commonalities and differences can be shown between nurses' subjective concepts of prevention and what they relate about how to put concepts of prevention into practice in their day-to-day work.

LEVELS OF LINKING QUALITATIVE AND QUANTITATIVE RESEARCH

In mixing qualitative and quantitative research, the question arises as to which level the mix concretely addresses. Here we have two alternatives. Combinations of qualitative and quantitative research can be applied to the single case. The same persons who are interviewed are also members of the sample who fill in a questionnaire. Their answers to questions in both methods are compared, brought together and related to each other at the level of the single case as well. Sampling decisions are taken in two steps. The same cases are selected for both parts of the study, but in a second step it is decided which of the participants are selected for an interview. The link can be established in addition – or only – at the level of datasets. The answers to the questionnaire are analyzed in their frequency and distribution over the whole sample. The answers to the interview are analyzed and compared and a typology is developed. Then the distribution of answers from the questionnaire is linked to the typology and compared with it (see Figure 8.1). This can be employed in a similar way to combine two qualitative methods.

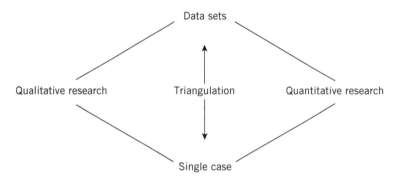

FIGURE 8.1 Levels of triangulation of qualitative and quantitative research

COMPUTERS IN STUDIES USING TRIANGULATION OR MIXED METHODS

QDA software

In the meantime, not only for quantitative data, for which SPSS has become a standard software, but also for qualitative data, a number of software programs are available, mostly **QDA** (qualitative data analysis) **software** (see also Gibbs, 2018, for more details). These programs are designed to support the analysis of textual data (interviews, conversation transcripts) and visual material (images, film, video). The most important programs are ATLAS.ti, NVivo, and **MAXQDA** (see Gibbs, 2018, for details). In contrast to SPSS they do not perform the analysis or the analytical steps themselves but they support the management of texts or images and the retrieval and coding of material. Thus they are more like a word processor than a statistics program. For applying such programs in the context of a study using triangulation and mixed methods, we can discuss several problems.

Administration of and links between different sets of data

In using different sorts of data (e.g. interviews and focus groups), we face the problem of how to administer them. In the ATLAS.ti program, for example, hermeneutic units are built for an analysis. They include the primary texts (the data) and secondary texts (memos, codes, networks of codes, texts written during the analysis, etc.). These are linked among each other and can be administered and processed in connected ways. The program does not care, of course, whether the primary data are of one sort (interviews) or different sorts of data (interviews and focus group transcripts). However, they should be labelled specifically so that it will be possible later on to see whether a statement comes from an interview or from a focus group. If both parts of the study are analyzed separately first, it may be useful to set up different hermeneutic units for each of the parts to avoid the files becoming too big. It has proved difficult to merge several hermeneutic units. Therefore you should consider handling all the data (sorts) in one such unit right away, especially in studies triangulating methods for data collection. For within-method triangulation (for example, for the episodic interview) – the question may arise of how to code the various sorts of data (narratives and interviews) in a formal way to represent their distinctiveness. In programs like ATLAS.ti as well as in grounded theory research, which was used as a model for developing the program, codes address above all the contents of a text, so that the formal quality of a sequence is a second level of coding. Here you should define how to double code material right from the beginning of a study using triangulation.

Interfaces between QDA and statistics software

In studies using triangulation with qualitative and quantitative methods, the question arises of how to link the data and analyses referring to them at the level of the computer also. None of the QDA programs aims at or offers tools for statistical analyses within the program. SPSS is not set up for management and analysis of textual data (at the level of text, i.e. without coding in numbers). Therefore, different programs are used for the standardized and non-standardized parts of a study. This leads to questions of interfaces: can both program types be linked, can data and analyses done with ATLAS.ti, for example, be transferred into SPSS? The more recent versions of the programs offer such an option in both directions, which means they allow inclusion of information coming from SPSS. Here again, we should think about how to avoid any requirements coming from the program influencing data and analyses. This discussion has been going on for a while for the QDA programs in some detail. Empirical studies, however, have demonstrated that the types of analysis have not been reduced to specific methods because of the use of computers (see Fielding and Lee, 1998). More concrete examples of how to import demographic data (from SPSS) into analyses with NVivo can be found in Bazeley (2010). Fielding and Fielding (2015) discuss the use of QDA software in mixed methods research in particular, for including spatial data.

POSITION OF TRIANGULATION OR MIXED METHODS IN THE RESEARCH PROCESS

Exploration

As the preceding chapters have shown, triangulation or mixed methods can be used for different purposes and in different steps in the research process of qualitative research. For example, we can find from time to time that focus groups are used to explore the research issue. The results from the focus groups in such a case are only used for preparing the actual data collection in, for example, semi-structured interviews or questionnaires but not as a stand-alone part of the study or the overall results. Participant observation can also be a fruitful approach for exploring a field in which subsequent interviews or questionnaires are then applied.

Data collection

Furthermore, various methods of data collection can be combined. To remain in the example, semi-structured single interviews and focus groups are done that address different aspects of the issue. The data are then analyzed using the same method (for example, theoretical coding according to Glaser and Strauss, 1967). The different data are perhaps brought together in one set of data. Triangulation then remains limited to data collection. The mixing of qualitative and quantitative methods can also be limited to data collection, whereas analysis is pursued in independent legs of the project.

Data analysis

In a similar way, we can triangulate different methods of data interpretation by using it for data collected with one method. An example is to use (open or axial) coding according to Strauss (1987) in combination with applying a hermeneutic method to selected excerpts from a narrative interview. In their book, Wertz et al. (2011) take one interview and analyse it using five different methods (among them grounded theory, discourse analysis and narrative research). They show the differences and similarities in analyzing the text that the different methods produce. Here, the triangulation remains restricted to the step of analyzing the data. In a similar way, we can use it in both steps when we use different techniques for analyzing data collected using different methods.

Generalization

Another purpose for using triangulation or mixed methods can be the generalization of results. Whereas, for quantitative research, generalization is mainly a numerical problem, to be solved by statistical means, this issue is more complicated for qualitative research. For a start, the issue of generalization comes up in a similar way: a limited number of cases selected according to certain criteria (sometimes only one case) have been studied. The results claim validity beyond the material (cases, etc.) included in the study. Cases, groups, and so on in the study represent something more general. The issue of generalization comes up in qualitative research often in a fundamentally different way, as a part of this research is aimed at developing grounded theories from empirical material. Then generalization addresses the question: to which other contexts can the developed theory be transferred or for which other contexts is it valid beyond the one it was discovered in? Therefore, an approach for assessing qualitative research (pursuing this aim) is to ask which considerations and steps were undertaken to define and perhaps to extend the area of validity of empirical results or theories developed from them.

A starting point for this assessment is to reflect on how the researchers analyzed their cases and how they proceeded from their cases to more general statements. The special problem of generalization for qualitative research is that its starting point is often an analysis that is referred to a context, one specific case in this context, and the conditions, relations and processes in it. This reference to context (often) gives qualitative research its specific significance. In generalization, this reference to a context is given up so as to analyze how far the results are valid independently and beyond specific contexts. In tackling this dilemma, Lincoln and Guba (1985) address this issue under the headline: 'The only generalization is: there is no generalization'.

However, they outline criteria and ways for generalizing insights beyond one context, when they suggest criteria such as the transferability of results from one context to another and fittingness as the degrees of comparability across different contexts.

Different ways and means are discussed for how to mark out the road from the case to the theory in such a way that at least a certain generalization can be reached. A first step is to clarify the question of what degree of generalization is intended with the single study at all and what can be reached, so that appropriate claims for generalization can be derived. A second step is to carefully include different cases and contexts, in which the issues are analyzed empirically. Generalizability of results is often closely linked to realizing the sample. Theoretical sampling offers a strategy for designing the variation of conditions, under which a phenomenon is studied, as broadly as possible. The third starting point is the systematic comparison of the collected materials. Triangulation or mixed methods can contribute to generalization in this sense. Here, the aim of triangulation is to transfer the results obtained at one level (e.g. knowledge) to a different level (e.g. practices) by using a second method of data collection. Seen more generally, when combining different (e.g. qualitative and quantitative) methods, it should be sorted out which logic (numerical or theoretical) generalization in the study should follow, and how far each approach to generalization can be transferred from one method to the other.

CONCLUSION

In summary, planning a study using triangulation or mixed methods comes with various problems. They are located between several aspects: a sufficiently consistent application of a combination of different methodological backgrounds, and a treatment of both approaches in the design and planning of the study with equal weight for both methods. The question is whether the efforts of triangulation or using mixed methods are in a sound relation to the advantages for answering the research question or promoting the quality of the research, and finally to the available resources. If these aspects are sufficiently considered, triangulation and mixed methods are worthwhile strategies for extending the knowledge potential compared to single-method studies. The advantages can be seen in two respects: (1) they produce far more profound, detailed and comprehensive results; (2) because of this, they are a strategy for advancing qualitative research by revealing the limits of single methods (or approaches) and by overcoming them.

Similar to what has been outlined in this chapter, Creswell (2015, p. 83) sees three possible locations of integration of qualitative and quantitative approaches in a mixed methods study: data collection, data analysis and the results section. Here he mentions four types of integration: merging the data when data are brought together in a convergent design; explanation of the data, when qualitative data explain the results of the quantitative analysis; building of the data, i.e. the qualitative results are used for developing the quantitative part; and embedding the data, when qualitative data are added to a quantitative design (2015, p. 83).

Perhaps we can end this brief overview of the use of triangulation and mixed methods as strategies for advancing qualitative research with two quotations, marking the tensional field in which triangulation is located:

There is no magic in triangulation. (Patton, 1980, p. 330)

Triangulation is expensive. Weak designs may result from its implementation. However, its use, when coupled with sophisticated rigor, will broaden, thicken, and deepen the interpretive base of any study. (Denzin, 1989, p. 247)

The same can be said about using mixed methods.

KEY POINTS

- Triangulation or mixed methods can be approaches for extending the insights from qualitative research.
- They come with some (extra) practical problems resulting from the different logical methods (or approaches) that are combined.
- Triangulation and mixed methods are not necessary in every study, but if one of them is used the practical problems mentioned here need some attention and then the method can be helpful.

FURTHER READING

In the following texts practical problems in general and when using triangulation or mixed methods are discussed in more detail:

Creswell, J.W. (2015) *A Concise Introduction to Mixed Methods Research*. Los Angeles, CA: Sage.
Denzin, N.K. (1989) *The Research Act*, 3rd ed. Englewood Cliffs, NJ: Prentice-Hall.
Flick, U. (2014) *An Introduction to Qualitative Research*, 5th ed. London: Sage.
Flick, U. (2018) *Designing Qualitative Research* (Book 1 of *The SAGE Qualitative Research Kit*, 2nd ed.). London: Sage.

CHAPTER NINE

SENSITIVE USE OF MULTIPLE METHODS

QUALITY, WRITING, AND ETHICS

CONTENTS

CHAPTER OBJECTIVES

After reading this chapter, you should know about:

- issues concerning sensitive use of triangulation and mixed methods;
- how quality criteria for using triangulation and mixed methods are discussed;
- which ethical issues arise and are discussed for the use of multiple methods;
- what the challenges are in writing about studies combining several approaches; and
- how these issues are interlinked.

QUALITY CRITERIA FOR STUDIES USING TRIANGULATION

Although triangulation was often mainly considered in the context of how to use it for advancing the quality of qualitative research, we can also ask the question the other way around: what constitutes the quality of a study using triangulation, and how can it be assessed? If we want to assess a study using triangulation or its planning, we can think of different aspects.

Compatibility of criteria

First of all, we have to consider for studies combining, for example, qualitative and quantitative methods that the quality criteria in each area cannot simply be applied to the other. In a consistent triangulation or mix of both approaches, we should avoid the assessment of the whole study being dominated by one of the approaches (and its criteria). We should try to also take the particularity of both approaches into account for using criteria or for quality assessment in general. There is a very limited consensus about quality and criteria inside qualitative research among different researchers and research perspectives (e.g. Sparkes, 2001, for the concept of validity). Accordingly, we should consider the perhaps different claims for quality in each approach when we combine several qualitative methods and also the appropriateness of the criteria in each case.

Quality of studies using triangulation

To answer the question what constitutes the quality of studies using triangulation, we should first consider if and how far the combination of different methods has taken into account the theoretical and methodological background of each method. Second, we should look at the relation in which the single methods were placed towards each other: have they been used on an equal footing, or was one used only in an exploratory way and the other as the main method? Third, we should see whether each method was used and treated by itself in a consistent way. Finally, it should become clear for any study using triangulation why the extra effort of using different methods was made, and that they accessed different levels and aspects of the phenomenon under study (see also Flick, 2018a, for a more detailed discussion of this aspect).

CRITERIA IN MIXED METHODS

In the context of mixed methods, the discussion of appropriate criteria for evaluating studies is livelier than in the area of triangulation. Greene (2007, p. 166–7) makes a common distinction by judging between the quality of method and data and the quality of inferences. One approach is to define common criteria for both types of research in mixed methods research, e.g. validity, which mainly refer to the connection of qualitative and quantitative parts of the study and the conclusions drawn from this (Creswell and Plano Clark, 2011, p. 239). However, the major problem for developing a consensual set of criteria here is outlined by Dellinger and Leech, who see that the terms qualitative and quantitative research reduce two complex ideas to two simple terms, but then continue to use these terms (2007, p. 309). Bryman (2006b, p. 122) discusses three ways in which quality criteria should be used in mixed methods research: (1) *convergent criteria*, i.e. the same criteria for the quantitative and qualitative components; (2) *separate criteria* – for each component; and (3) *bespoke criteria* – specifically for mixed methods research. Collins (2015) has looked at the discussion about criteria in mixed methods, starting from the following assumption: 'A critical dimension of high-quality research is to establish quality criteria for assessing the degree that the process *and* the outcome of the research are interpreted as credible, defensible, and rigorous' (p. 245). She discusses the issue of validity for the three paradigms (quantitative, qualitative, mixed methods). For quantitative approaches she discusses design and measurement validity. In her presentation, it becomes clear that criteria such as validity or reliability in quantitative research are more or less consensual across various scientific schools and methodological approaches. For qualitative research, she discusses suggestions for criteria such as those by Maxwell (validity – 1992) and Lincoln and Guba (**credibility**, authenticity, reflexivity – 1985). For mixed methods she discusses 'integrative efficacy' (pp. 247–8) as the main criterion for judging whether the study integrates approaches and findings of both legs of a mixed methods research study.

Whereas the discussion about criteria and quality claims in quantitative research is marked by a far-reaching consensus that reliability, validity and objectivity should be applied, the situation in qualitative research is different. Not only are these criteria rejected by many qualitative researchers and approaches as inadequate for qualitative research, but also there has been long and intense discussion about which criteria are adequate in general (see also Flick, 2018a): 'However, it is unlikely, given the controversy that has surrounded criteria in qualitative research (e.g. Sparkes, 2001), that, at least in the near future, criteria could be developed that would satisfy the qualitative research community' (Bryman, 2006b, p. 123). Thus it is unlikely that the first two alternatives Bryman sees for applying criteria to mixed methods research (convergent and separate criteria) will lead to a generally shared understanding of quality in mixed methods research (or the triangulation of qualitative and quantitative research). The way out discussed in the field of mixed methods research is what Bryman (2006b) labels as 'bespoke criteria for mixed-methods research' based on the notion of *inference quality*. Teddlie and Tashakkori (2009, pp. 301–2) have suggested an 'integrative framework for inference quality', which they group around two aspects of quality. *Design quality* refers to (1) design suitability (appropriateness), (2) design fidelity (adequacy), (3) within-design consistency and (4) analytic adequacy. *Interpretive rigour* refers to (5) interpretive consistency, (6) theoretical consistency, (7) interpretive agreement, (8) interpretive distinctiveness, (9) integrative efficacy and (10) interpretive correspondence. This suggestion heavily focuses on aspects such as consistency rather than diversity in results, on technical aspects of design rather than the appropriateness of using mixed methods, and thus reduces mixed methods research to some kind of confirmatory approach with several datasets (which was for a long time misassociated with triangulation in distinction to other aims of using multiple methods). Dellinger and Leech (2007, p. 320) accordingly transform the criteria issue (what is good mixed methods research?) into an interaction problem and a consensus process developed around construct validation: 'We propose that construct validation is the continuous process of negotiation of meaning. This is accomplished through argument as dialogue, criticism, and objection'. To turn the quality issue of mixed methods research into a communication problem between the researchers (or approaches) involved is one side of the problem. The other side becomes evident when the quality of mixed methods research is judged from outside – for example, in reviews of using mixed methods research in a field such as health services research. O'Cathain et al. (2008, pp. 96–7) identified a lack of **transparency** in presenting the mixed methods aspects, and poor descriptions of qualitative strands in the overall presentation of such studies. O'Cathain (2010) extends this discussion and again discusses three approaches – a generic approach, an individual component and a mixed methods approach. Whereas the first one builds on the assumption that general criteria should also apply to mixed methods research, the second one focuses on differences between the qualitative and quantitative parts of a mixed methods research study and the third one asks for specific criteria for mixed methods research. In her own framework she nails down the quality question to steps such as planning a mixed methods research study, undertaking it, interpreting the findings, dissemination and application in the real world (2010, pp. 540–5). Finally, she identifies as a problem that there are too many criteria in the discussion rather than a lack of criteria.

Resuming this short overview of the criteria discussion in mixed methods research, we can see two major problems. (1) There is not really a consensus about how to deal with the differing discussions in both 'paradigms', which allows developing of consistent criteria for the 'new paradigm'. (2) The criteria problem tends to be transformed to a communicative problem/process among the researchers and even more between the researchers and their audiences. This demonstrates how closely interlinked issues of writing about mixed methods research and the quality of mixed methods research are.

CRITERIA FOR USING COMBINATIONS OF QUALITATIVE AND QUANTITATIVE RESEARCH

Combinations of qualitative and quantitative research are also used more and more often in the context of advancing qualitative research. Some methodological questions about this use have not been answered in a satisfactory way. A series of approaches of combining both exist, in which sometimes the systematic or the methodological level is secondary to pragmatics concerning research practices or concepts. Attempts to integrate both often lead to the use of one after the other (with different ways of sequencing), side by side (with different degrees of independence for both strategies) or in super- or subordination (in either direction). Integration often concentrates on linking the results or on the level of research designs – a combinatory use of different methods with different degrees of reference to each other. Furthermore, the differences between both strategies continue to exist for assessing procedure, data and results. The question of how to take this into account in the combination of both strategies should be further discussed, and in particular when this combination is used for advancing qualitative research.

There are some guiding questions for assessing examples of combining qualitative and quantitative research (see also Flick, 2014a, Chapter 3):

- Are both approaches given an equal weight (in the plan of the project, in the relevance of the results and in judging the quality of the research, for example)?
- Are both approaches just applied separately or are they really related to each other? For example, many studies use qualitative and quantitative methods rather independently and in the end the integration of both parts only refers to comparing the results of both.
- What is the logical relation of both? Are they only sequenced, and if so, how? Or are they really integrated in a multi-methods design?
- What are the criteria used for evaluating the research all in all? Is there domination of a traditional view of validation or are both forms of research evaluated using appropriate criteria?

If we take the issues mentioned in these guiding questions into account, triangulation of qualitative and quantitative research can contribute to advancing qualitative research and the quality of its outcomes. Like other strategies and approaches mentioned in this book, it is not the one and only way to go about using quantitative approaches in qualitative research and is by no means appropriate in every project. Here, even more than in the other examples, the question of indications for methods (see the end of this chapter) needs particular attention.

WRITING ABOUT USING MULTIPLE METHODS

Bazeley (2015) discusses a number of tensions and practical problems in writing about mixed methods research projects. These include philosophical–epistemological differences behind the approaches or interdisciplinary and methodological tensions as well as differing ideas about how to write and what research quality is about. These tensions are not only relevant for writing about mixed methods research but also for doing it and for integrating the concepts of research behind the two legs of a mixed methods research project. More specific are problems linked to the targets of writing – the academic or non-academic audiences who need to understand a mixed methods research project and procedure and the limitations coming from journal article (length) limitations, which are often difficult to meet with a mono method study.

Presentation of studies using mixed methods research

Morse and Maddox (2014) present a number of suggestions for how to integrate qualitative and quantitative findings (and procedures) in a mixed methods research project.

Their focus is on the use of diagramming of the procedures and of the findings to make the whole process and its outcomes more transparent for readers. Dickinson (2010) discusses other forms of visual displays for mixed methods research findings. As in other approaches (see Flick, 2014a, Chapter 30) writing about mixed methods research is not just the presentation of findings, but is closely interlinked with doing the research and with making its quality accessible. The relevance of these interconnections and of the step of presenting the research becomes evident in the analysis of O'Cathain et al. (2008, p. 97) in the field of health services research (HSR) and the mixed methods research therein (see above). In consequence, they suggest guidelines including aspects such as the justification of using mixed methods because of the research question as well as describing design and each method (sampling, collection and analysis of data). It should become clear where and how the integration was realized, and what the limitations and major insights of a mixed approach were in the study.

Presentation of studies using triangulation

For the presentation of results and procedures in studies using triangulation, several general problems, which are known for presenting qualitative research in general, occur again but more seriously. First, an understandable and straightforward presentation, that is, one that is appropriate to the potential reader in its length, is much more difficult than for quantitative studies, if we want to present not only results but also the ways in which we produced them (see Lüders, 2004b). Quantitative results can be more easily presented in the form of tables, numbers and distributions. At the same time, quantitative results are often processed at a much higher level of aggregation than in qualitative research. In surveys, you will rarely work with results at the level of the single case, whereas in qualitative research the case study is often the first step and a comparative analysis only the second step when presenting the research.

The first necessity for presenting a study using triangulation seems to be to make the different methodological procedures in themselves understandable and also to show how the triangulation was applied concretely, and finally to give examples of how results have been linked. In the end, the presentation should make clear why triangulation was used and why it was appropriate and necessary (see Gibbs, 2018; Rapley, 2018).

ETHICAL ISSUES OF USING MULTIPLE METHODS

With respect to research ethics in mixed methods research, again the discussion oscillates between positions that the same ethical issues are relevant as in other forms of social research and that it is time for 'putting ethics on the mixed methods map' (Preissle et al., 2015) as there are a number of special challenges on the ethical level. The first is how to justify the use of several methodological approaches and applying them to the same participants or fields. Just the belief that mixed methods research is per se better than a single-method approach may not be enough to justify extra contributions by the participants (an interview *and* a questionnaire to be answered): what is the extra value from using multiple methods? (Preissle et al., 2015, p. 147). The second is how to deal with potential over-challenges in applying the methods to the participants – what are points to keep in mind? The third is how to keep issues of anonymity and data protection in mind, if several methodological approaches reveal a fuller picture of the participant – in particular in the display and discussion of results. What are the ethical issues in the relationship between the researcher and participants? Preissle et al. emphasize the need for (more) transparency in and about mixed methods research (see above) procedures and results, and resume their overview: 'While the practice of mixed methods research has grown tremendously over the past decades, dialogue about related ethical issues has been neglected' (2015, p. 158).

Most of these issues also apply to using triangulation (of several qualitative approaches) as well. Some become even more relevant as the insights and interventions in everyday life circumstances of the participants are even more comprehensive if an interview is combined with participant observation, for example, and not with a questionnaire (as in a mixed methods research study). Here again, a specific ethical sensitivity is necessary reflecting on why and how multiple methods are applied and what is reported from the study and how.

HOW: QUALITY, TRANSPARENCY, ETHICS

The brief remarks in this chapter emphasize how the issues of quality in using multiple methods, of writing about how research was done and of making transparent how far it was done in an ethically justified and justifiable way are interlinked. Coming back to the beginning of this chapter, a solution for how to address the quality of using multiple (mixed or triangulated) methods in a study could be to orient on discussions about what Tracy (2010) has suggested as the eight 'big tent' criteria for qualitative research. With the term 'big tent criteria' she refers to the fact that the criteria do not refer to a single step in the research process. In a validity check in a quantitative study, the validity of the measurement is assessed. Other aspects such as whether the study has addressed a relevant issue at all are ignored in such a quality assessment. Tracy includes such aspects and defines her criteria as follows: 'high quality qualitative methodological research is marked by (a) worthy topic, (b) rich rigor, (c) sincerity, (d) credibility, (e) resonance, (f) significant contribution, (g) ethics, and (h) meaningful coherence' (2010, p. 839). Her more detailed description of these criteria includes, for example for 'worthy topic': 'The topic of the research is relevant; timely; significant; interesting' (p. 840). 'Rich rigor' refers to: 'The study uses sufficient, abundant, appropriate, and complex theoretical constructs; data and time in the field; sample(s); context(s); data collection and analysis processes' (2010, p. 841). The criterion 'credibility' comprises strategies such as triangulation, member checks and the treatment of **deviant case**s (discussed as 'multivocality') (2010, p. 844). To integrate ethics in such an approach to quality assessment as well as to emphasize worthy topics and meaningful coherence brings the overall justification of a specific (multiple methods) approach onto the agenda and allows a more comprehensive assessment of the integrity of a project. For all these issues, it is central to reflect on why and when to use mixed methods or triangulation: why is it necessary, what extra gain in knowledge is possible using this way, etc.? Good ways of using mixed methods research and triangulation should be characterized by a systematic use of different methods or methods with different approaches (not just interviews and questionnaires, for example). Also they should include the integration and reflection of theoretical backgrounds of different methods in approaching their field. A central criterion can be how far the concrete project includes methods that are approaching different levels or dimensions of the issue under study. Examples of such different levels are to study subjective meaning and social structures of a problem or to analyze process and state in the empirical data or knowledge and practices on the part of the participants. The basic quality feature is the purposeful choice and use of methods that are combined.

WHY AND WHEN: INDICATIONS FOR APPROACHES AND DESIGNS

Why do we use a specific method of qualitative research for studying a specific issue? Why, and in particular, when do we use a specific combination of methods in a concrete study? Is it always the appropriateness of methods to issues that drives us in our decision for one method and against other ones, or for a combination of a certain kind? Is this relation of appropriateness so clearly defined that it makes decisions easy, clear and obvious? Or do many of our colleagues not simply do what they always did: do they not just simply continue with methods they used before when they start a new project? In particular, in times of euphoria linked to approaches such as mixed methods research, this danger seems quite relevant, as Bryman's (2007) results have shown. It is often not the research question that drives the decision for using mixed methods research or not, but the habit and the general belief in the superiority of this approach. Perhaps a look at the life record of social researchers and the methods they used over the years will show a limited variation in the application of methods in many cases. These questions bring us to how to make the decision for a specific method and/or a specific research design more explicit. In methodology discussions mainly in textbooks, research methods are mostly focused on as side by side issues for describing their features, advantages and problems. A comparative perspective, which would give the reader a rationale for deciding when to use this method or design and when not to use it, is seldom taken. Such a comparative perspective can be taken by questioning the indication for a specific method (or methods combination) for a particular study. Indication in social research means basically three things, if we look at it from the angle of appropriateness of research approaches. (1) To select the appropriate method by taking into account to whom or what it shall be applied. (2) To document this selection process and the decisions taken in it and why they were taken. (3) And finally, to make this process transparent to the reader or consumer of the research (see Flick, 2014a, Chapter 29, which spells out this idea in more detail for qualitative research). The core of this is how to select a research method and in particular how to decide whether or not to use combinations of methods and which ones. This will avoid automatisms on two sides: first, the researchers who decide to subscribe to mixed methods research without asking why they should use it but only focusing on how to design it; second, the funders and users of research who might overestimate the potentials of mixed methods research for each and every issue; both might return to more realistic expectations about what research approaches can deliver.

● KEY POINTS

- Definitions of research quality and of criteria in mixed methods and triangulation oscillate between taking criteria from one approach and applying them to a combined approach, and defining specific criteria for the latter.
- Assessing the justification and quality of mixed methods and triangulation has a lot to do with the transparency of the selection and application of the approaches, and thus is closely linked to writing about the research.
- Research ethics in this context include some additional challenges compared to other forms of research (such as the justification for choosing a triangulation or mixed methods approach or the practical and ethical implications for those who participate).
- Bringing these issues together suggests a 'big tent' approach to assessing quality rather than seeing this a technical problem and assessing single steps of applying methods.

FURTHER READING

In these sources, the discussion about combining qualitative and quantitative research or several qualitative approaches is continued without falling into euphoria about mixing methods on a pragmatic level to make it fruitful for advancing qualitative research:

Flick, U. (2014) *An Introduction to Qualitative Research*, 5th ed. London: Sage, Chapter 3.

Flick, U. (2017) 'Mantras and myths: the disenchantment of mixed-methods research and revisiting triangulation as a perspective', *Qualitative Inquiry*, 23 (1): 48–56.

Flick, U. (2018) 'Triangulation', in N.K. Denzin and Y.S. Lincoln (eds), *The SAGE Handbook of Qualitative Research*, 5th ed. London and Thousand Oaks, CA: Sage, pp. 444–61.

Preissle, J., Glover-Kudon, R.M., Rohan, E.A., Boehm, J.E. and DeGroff, A. (2015) 'Putting ethics on the mixed methods map', in S.N. Hesse-Biber and B. Johnson (eds), *The Oxford Handbook of Multimethod and Mixed Methods Research Inquiry*. Oxford: Oxford University Press, pp. 144–63.

GLOSSARY

ATLAS.ti Software for supporting the qualitative analysis of text, images and other data in qualitative research.

Between-methods triangulation Combination of two independent methods in studying one issue.

Bias Disturbing influence on research and results.

Communicative validation Assessment of results (or of data) by asking the participants for their consensus.

Comprehensive triangulation Combination of the different forms of triangulation (investigator, theory, methods and data) in one mode.

Credibility Criterion for evaluating qualitative research based on prolonged engagement in the field.

Criteria Instruments for assessing the quality of research, ideally coming with a cut-off point (benchmark), to distinguish good from bad research.

Data triangulation Combination of different forms of data.

Deviant case Case not fitting in or supporting a model or other forms of findings.

Episodic interview Interview combining question–answer sequences with narratives (of episodes).

Evaluation   Use of research methods for estimating and deciding about the success of an intervention.

Evidence-based practices   Interventions (in medicine, social work, nursing, etc.) that are based on results of research.

Falsification   Testing theories by trying to show that they are not correct.

Generalization   Transfer of research results to situations and populations that were not part of the research situation.

Hybrid methodologies   Methodologies that include elements from more than one method or approach (e.g. in ethnography).

Hypothesis   In standardized research, assumptions to be tested in research. In qualitative research, hypotheses are used in a more metaphorical sense (e.g. as working hypotheses) without being formulated before the research and being tested.

Indication   Decision about when exactly (under which conditions) a specific method (or combination of methods) should be used.

Informed consent   Participants in a study are informed that they are to be studied and are given the chance to say no to the research.

Investigator triangulation   Combination of more than one researcher either in collaboration or independently to promote the quality of the research.

Likert scale   Questions in a questionnaire with five (sometimes seven) standardized alternatives for answers, which can be ticked by the respondent.

MAXQDA   Software for analyzing qualitative data; earlier versions were called WinMax.

Member checks   Assessment of results (or of data) by asking the participants for their consensus.

Mixed methods/methodologies   An approach combining qualitative and quantitative methods at a rather pragmatic level.

Narrative-episodic knowledge   Knowledge based on memories of situations and their concrete circumstances.

NVivo Software for analyzing qualitative data; earlier versions were called 'Nudist'.

Objectivity The degree to which a research situation (the application of methods and their outcome) is independent of the individual researcher.

Proposal Research plan developed for applying for funding or in a PhD or master's programme.

QDA software Qualitative data analysis software specially developed to support the analysis of texts like interviews and their coding, administration, etc. Examples are ATLAS.ti, MAXQDA and NVivo.

Quality of life A concept for analyzing the situation of living in the context of an illness or a treatment, mostly measured using standardized instruments like the SF-36.

Reliability One of the standard criteria in standardized/quantitative research, measured, for example, by repeating a test and assessing whether the results are the same in both cases.

Research design A systematic plan for a research project, including who to integrate in the research (sampling), who or what to compare for which dimensions, etc.

Sampling The selection of cases, persons, materials, etc., to study from a bigger population or variety.

Semantic-conceptual knowledge Knowledge organized around concepts, their meaning and relations among each other.

SF-36 A standard questionnaire for analyzing quality of life in the context of a health problem or treatment.

Social representations A concept for describing the knowledge of social groups about scientific findings or other issues.

Subjective theory Laypeople's knowledge about certain issues can be organized similarly to scientific theories (e.g. subjective theories of health or illness).

Systematic triangulation of perspectives The combination of different methods including their (differing) theoretical backgrounds in the study of one issue.

Theoretical sampling   The sampling procedure in grounded theory research, where cases, groups or materials are sampled according to their relevance for the theory that is developed and against the background of what is already the state of knowledge after collecting and analyzing a certain number of cases.

Theory triangulation   The combination of different theoretical perspectives in the study of one issue.

Transparency   The degree to which a reader of a research study is enabled to understand how the research went on in concrete terms.

Triangulation   The combination of different methods, theories, data and/or researchers in the study of one issue.

Triathlon   An extreme kind of sport combining running a marathon, swimming and cycling very long distances.

Validity   One of the standard criteria in standardized/quantitative research, analyzed for example by looking for confounding influences (internal validity) or for transferability to situations beyond the current research situation (external validity).

Within-method triangulation   The combination of two methodological approaches (e.g. question–answer and narratives) in one method.

REFERENCES

Amann, K. and Hirschauer, S. (1997) 'Die Befremdung der eigenen Kultur. Ein Programm', in S. Hirschauer and K. Amann (eds), *Die Befremdung der eigenen Kultur. Zur ethnogra phischen Herausforderung soziologischer Empirie*. Frankfurt a. M.: Suhrkamp, pp. 7–52.

Archibald, M.M. (2015) 'Investigator triangulation: a collaborative strategy with potential for mixed methods research', *Journal of Mixed Methods Research*, 10 (3): 228–50.

Atkinson, P., Coffey, A., Delamont, S., Lofland, J. and Lofland, L. (eds) (2001) *Handbook of Ethnography*. London: Sage.

Baker, S.E. and Edwards, R. (2012) *How Many Qualitative Interviews Is Enough?* Discussion Paper. NCRM. http://eprints.ncrm.ac.uk/2273.

Banks, M. (2018) *Using Visual Data in Qualitative Research* (Book 5 of *The SAGE Qualitative Research Kit*, 2nd ed.). London: Sage.

Barbour, R. (2018) *Doing Focus Groups* (Book 4 of *The SAGE Qualitative Research Kit*, 2nd ed.). London: Sage.

Barton, A.H. and Lazarsfeld, P.F. (1955) 'Some functions of qualitative analysis in social research', in *Frankfurter Beiträge zur Soziologie I*. Frankfurt a. M.: Europäische Verlagsanstalt, pp. 321–61.

Bateson, G. and Mead, M. (1942) *Balinese Character: A Photographic Analysis*, Vol. 2. New York: New York Academy of Sciences.

Bazeley, P. (2010) 'Computer assisted integration of mixed methods data sources and anal-yses', in A. Tashakkori and C. Teddlie (eds), *The SAGE Handbook of Mixed Methods in Social and Behavioral Research*, 2nd ed. Thousand Oaks, CA: Sage, pp. 431–67.

Bazeley, P. (2015) 'Writing up multimethod and mixed methods research for diverse audi-ences', in S. Hesse-Biber and R.B. Johnson (eds), *The Oxford Handbook of Multimethod and Mixed Method Research Inquiry*. Oxford: Oxford University Press, pp. 296–313.

Becker, H. and Geer, B.S. (1960) 'Participant observation: analysis of qualitative data', in R.N. Adams and J.J. Preiss (eds), *Human Organization Research*. Homewood, IL: Dorsey Press, pp. 267–89.

Bergmann, J.R. (1985) 'Flüchtigkeit und methodische Fixierung sozialer Wirklichkeit. Aufzeichnungen als Daten der interpretativen Soziologie', in W. Bonss and H. Hartmann (eds), *Entzauberte Wissenschaft – Zur Realität und Geltung soziologischer Forschung*. Göttingen: Schwartz, pp. 299–320.

Blaikie, N.W. (1991) 'A critique of the use of triangulation in social research', *Quality and Quantity*, 25: 115–36.

Brewer, J. and Hunter, A. (1989) *Multimethod Research: A Synthesis of Styles*. Newbury Park, CA: Sage.

Brinkmann, S. and Kvale, S. (2018) *Doing Interviews* (Book 2 of *The SAGE Qualitative Research Kit*, 2nd ed.). London: Sage.

Bruner, J. (1990) *Acts of Meaning*. Cambridge, MA: Harvard University Press.

Bruner, J. (2002) *Making Stories: Law, Literature, Life*. Cambridge, MA: Harvard University Press.

Bryman, A. (1992) 'Quantitative and qualitative research: further reflections on their integration', in J. Brannen (ed.), *Mixing Methods: Quantitative and Qualitative Research*. Aldershot: Avebury, pp. 57–80.

Bryman, A. (2004) *Social Research Methods*, 2nd ed. Oxford: Oxford University Press.

Bryman, A. (2006a) 'Integrating quantitative and qualitative research: how is it done?', *Qualitative Research*, 6: 97–113.

Bryman, A. (2006b) 'Paradigm peace and the implications for quality', *International Journal of Social Research Methodology*, 9 (2): 111–26.

Bryman, A. (2007) 'The research question in social research: what is its role?', *International Journal of Social Research Methodology*, 10 (1): 5–20.

Campbell, D. and Fiske, D. (1959) 'Convergent and discriminant validation by the multitrait–multimethod matrix', *Psychological Bulletin*, 56: 81–105.

Clark, D. (1951) *Plane and Geodetic Surveying for Engineers*, Vol. 2. London: Constable.

Coffey, A. (2018) *Doing Ethnography* (Book 3 of *The SAGE Qualitative Research Kit*, 2nd ed.). London: Sage.

Collins, K.T. (2015) 'Validity in multimethod and mixed research', in S. Hesse-Biber and R.B. Johnson (eds), *The Oxford Handbook of Multimethod and Mixed Method Research Inquiry*. Oxford: Oxford University Press, pp. 240–56.

Cook, T.D. (1985) 'Postpositivist critical multiplism', in R.L. Shotland and M.M. Mark (eds), *Social Science and Social Policy*. Beverly Hills, CA: Sage, pp. 21–62.

Creswell, J.W. (2003) *Research Design: Qualitative, Quantitative, and Mixed Methods Approaches*. Thousand Oaks, CA: Sage.

Creswell, J.W. (2009) 'Editorial: mapping the field of mixed methods research', *Journal of Mixed Methods Research*, 3(2): 95–108.

Creswell, J.W. (2015) *A Concise Introduction to Mixed Methods Research*. Los Angeles, CA: Sage.

Creswell, J.W. and Plano Clark, V.L. (2007) *Designing and Conducting Mixed Methods Research.* Thousand Oaks, CA: Sage.

Creswell, J.W. and Plano Clark, V.L. (2011) *Designing and Conducting Mixed Methods Research,* 2nd ed. Thousand Oaks, CA: Sage.

Creswell, J.W., Plano Clark, V.L., Gutman, M.L. and Hanson, W.E. (2003) 'Advanced mixed methods research design', in A. Tashakkori and C. Teddlie (eds), *Handbook of Mixed Methods in Social and Behavioral Research.* Thousand Oaks, CA: Sage, pp. 209–40.

Dausien, B. and Kelle, H. (2003) 'Zur Verbindung von ethnographischen und biographischen Forschungsperspektiven', in J. Allmendinger (ed.), *Entstaatlichung und soziale Sicherheit,* CD-Supplement. Opladen: Leske & Budrich.

Dellinger, A.B and Leech, N.L. (2007) 'Toward a unified validation framework in mixed methods research', *Journal of Mixed Methods Research,* 1 (4): 309–32.

Denzin, N.K. (1970) *The Research Act.* Chicago: Aldine.

Denzin, N.K. (1989) *The Research Act,* 3rd ed. Englewood Cliffs, NJ: Prentice-Hall.

Denzin, N.K. (2004) 'Symbolic interactionism', in U. Flick, E. von Kardorff and I. Steinke (eds), *A Companion to Qualitative Research.* London: Sage, pp. 81–7.

Denzin, N.K. (2010) 'Moments, mixed methods, and paradigm dialogs', *Qualitative Inquiry,* 16 (6): 419–27.

Denzin, N.K (2012) 'Triangulation 2.0', *Journal of Mixed Methods Research,* 6: 80–8.

Denzin, N. and Lincoln, Y.S. (eds) (1994) *Handbook of Qualitative Research.* London: Sage.

Denzin, N. and Lincoln, Y.S. (eds) (2005) *The SAGE Handbook of Qualitative Research,* 3rd ed. London: Sage.

Dickinson, W.B. (2010) 'Visual displays for mixed methods findings', in A. Tashakkori and C. Teddlie (eds), *The SAGE Handbook of Mixed Methods in Social and Behavioral Research,* 2nd ed. Thousand Oaks, CA: Sage, pp. 469–504.

Ellingson, L.L. (2009) *Engaging Crystallization in Qualitative Research.* Thousand Oaks, CA: Sage.

Ellingson, L.L. (2011) 'Analysis and representation across the continuum', in N.K. Denzin and Y.S. Lincoln (eds), *The SAGE Handbook of Qualitative Research,* 4th ed. Thousand Oaks, CA: Sage, pp. 595–61.

Erzberger, C. and Kelle, U. (2003) 'Making inferences in mixed methods: the rules of integration', in A. Tashakkori, and C. Teddlie (eds), *Handbook of Mixed Methods in Social and Behavioral Research.* Thousand Oaks, CA: Sage, pp. 457–88.

Fielding, J.L. and Fielding, N.G. (2015) 'Emergent technologies in multimethod and mixed methods research: incorporating GIS and CAQDAS', in S. Hesse-Biber and R.B. Johnson (eds), *The Oxford Handbook of Multimethod and Mixed Method Research Inquiry.* Oxford: Oxford University Press, pp. 561–85.

Fielding, N.G. and Fielding, J.L. (1986) *Linking Data.* Beverly Hills, CA: Sage.

Fielding, N.G. and Lee, R.M. (1998) *Computer Analysis and Qualitative Research.* London: Sage.

Fleck, C. (2004) 'Marie Jahoda', in U. Flick, E. von Kardorff and I. Steinke (eds), *A Companion to Qualitative Research.* London: Sage, pp. 58–62.

Flick, U. (1992) 'Triangulation revisited: strategy of or alternative to validation of qualitative data?', *Journal for the Theory of Social Behavior*, 22: 175–97.

Flick, U. (1994) 'Social representations and the social construction of everyday knowledge: theoretical and methodological queries', *Social Science Information*, 35 (2): 179–97.

Flick, U. (1995) 'Social representations', in R. Harre, J. Smith and L. van Langenhove (eds), *Rethinking Psychology*. London: Sage, pp. 70–96.

Flick, U. (1996) *Psychologie des technisierten Alltags*. Opladen: Westdeutscher Verlag.

Flick, U. (ed.) (1998) *Psychology of the Social: Representations in Knowledge and Language*. Cambridge: Cambridge University Press.

Flick, U. (2000a) 'Episodic interviewing', in M. Bauer and G. Gaskell (eds), *Qualitative Researching with Text, Image and Sound: A Handbook*. London: Sage, pp. 75–92.

Flick, U. (2000b) 'Qualitative inquiries into social representations of health', *Journal of Health Psychology*, 5: 309–18.

Flick, U. (2004) 'Triangulation in qualitative research', in U. Flick, E. von Kardorff and I. Steinke (eds), *A Companion to Qualitative Research*. London: Sage, pp. 178–83.

Flick, U. (2005) 'Qualitative research in Germany and the US: state of the art, differences and developments', *FQS – Forum Qualitative Sozialforschung*, 6 (3). www.qualitative-research.net/index.php/fqs/article/view/17/37.

Flick, U. (2010) 'Triangulation of micro-perspectives on juvenile homelessness, health and human rights', in N. Denzin and M. Giardina (eds), *Qualitative Inquiry and Human Rights*. Walnut Creek, CA: Left Coast Press, pp. 186–204.

Flick, U. (2011) 'Mixing methods, triangulation and integrated research: challenges for qualitative research in a world of crisis', in N.K. Denzin and M. Giardina (eds), *Qualitative Inquiry and Global Crises*. Walnut Creek, CA: Left Coast Press, pp. 132–52.

Flick, U. (2012) 'Vulnerability and the politics of advocacy: challenges for qualitative inquiry using multiple methods', in N.K. Denzin and M. Giardina (eds), *Qualitative Inquiry and the Politics of Advocacy*. Walnut Creek, CA: Left Coast Press, pp. 163–82.

Flick, U. (2014a) *An Introduction to Qualitative Research*, 5th ed. London: Sage.

Flick, U. (ed.) (2014b) 'Special issue: challenges for qualitative inquiry as a global endeavor', *Qualitative Inquiry*, 20.

Flick, U. (2015) *Introducing Research Methodology – A Beginners' Guide to Doing a Research Project*, 2nd ed. London and Thousand Oaks, CA: Sage.

Flick, U. (2017) 'Mantras and myths: the disenchantment of mixed-methods research and revisiting triangulation as a perspective', *Qualitative Inquiry*, 23 (1): 46–58.

Flick, U. (2018a) *Managing Qualitative Research* (Book 10 of *The SAGE Qualitative Research Kit*, 2nd ed.). London: Sage.

Flick, U. (2018b) *Designing Qualitative Research* (Book 1 of *The SAGE Qualitative Research Kit*, 2nd ed.). London: Sage.

Flick, U. (2018c) 'Triangulation', in N.K. Denzin and Y.S. Lincoln (eds), *The SAGE Handbook of Qualitative Research*, 5th ed. London and Thousand Oaks, CA: Sage, pp. 444–61.

Flick, U. and Röhnsch, G. (2007) 'Idealisation and neglect: health concepts of homeless adolescents', *Journal of Health Psychology*, 12 (5): 737–50.

Flick, U., Garms-Homolová, V. and Röhnsch, G. (2010) '"When they sleep, they sleep": daytime activities and sleep disorders in nursing homes', *Journal of Health Psychology*, 15: 755–64.

Flick, U., Fischer, C., Neuber, A., Walter, U. and Schwartz F.W. (2003) 'Health in the context of being old – representations held by health professionals', *Journal of Health Psychology*, 8 (5): 539–56.

Flick, U., Walter, U., Fischer, C., Neuber, A. and Schwartz, F.-W. (2004) *Gesundheit als Leitidee? Gesundheitsvorstellungen von Ärzten und Pflegekräften*. Bern: Huber.

Flick, U., Garms-Homolová, V., Herrmann, W., Kuck, J. and Röhnsch, G. (2012) '"I can't prescribe something just because someone asks for it …": using mixed methods in the framework of triangulation', *Journal of Mixed Methods Research*, 6: 97–110.

Gebauer, G., Alkemeyer, T., Boschert, B., Flick, U. and Schmidt, R. (2004) *Treue zum Stil*. Bielefeld: Transcript.

Gibbs, G. (2018) *Analyzing Qualitative Data* (Book 6 of *The SAGE Qualitative Research Kit*, 2nd ed.). London: Sage.

Giddings, L.S. (2006) 'Mixed methods research: positivism dressed in drag?', *Journal of Research in Nursing*, 11 (3): 195–203.

Glaser, B.G. and Strauss, A.L. (1967) *The Discovery of Grounded Theory: Strategies for Qualitative Research*. New York: Aldine.

Goffmann, E. (1974) *Frame Analysis: An Essay on the Organization of Experience*. Cambridge, MA: Harvard University Press.

Goffman, E. (1989) 'On fieldwork', *Journal of Contemporary Ethnography*, 18: 123–32.

Greene, J.C. (2007) *Mixed Methods in Social Inquiry*. San Francisco, CA: Jossey-Bass.

Greene, J.C. (2008) 'Is mixed methods social inquiry a distinctive methodology?', *Journal of Mixed Methods Research*, 2: 7–22.

Greene, J. (2015) 'Preserving distinctions within the multimethod and mixed methods research merger', in S. Hesse-Biber and R.B. Johnson (eds), *The Oxford Handbook of Multimethod and Mixed Method Research Inquiry*. Oxford: Oxford University Press, pp. 606–15.

Greene, J.C. and Caracelli, V.J. (1997) 'Defining and describing the paradigm issues in mixed-method evaluation', in J.C. Greene and V.J. Caracelli (eds), *Advances in Mixed-Method Evaluation: The Challenges and Benefits of Integrating Diverse Paradigms*. San Francisco, CA: Jossey-Bass, pp. 5–18.

Greene, J. and Hall, J.N. (2010) 'Dialectics and pragmatism: being of consequence', in A. Tashakkori and C. Teddlie (eds), *The SAGE Handbook of Mixed Methods in Social and Behavioral Research*, 2nd ed. Thousand Oaks, CA: Sage, pp. 119–44.

Greene, J.C., Caracelli, V.J. and Graham, W.F. (1989) 'Toward a conceptual framework for mixed-method evaluation design', *Educational Evaluation and Policy Analysis*, 11 (3): 255–74.

Groeben, N. (1990) 'Subjective theories and the explanation of human action', in G.R. Semin and K.J. Gergen (eds), *Everyday Understanding: Social and Scientific Implications.* London: Sage, pp. 19–44.

Guest, G. (2013) 'Describing mixed methods research: an alternative to typologies', *Journal of Mixed Methods Research*, 7 (2): 141–51.

Guggenmoos-Holzmann, I., Bloomfield, K., Brenner, H. and Flick, U. (eds) (1995) *Quality of Life and Health: Concepts, Methods and Applications.* Oxford: Blackwell Science.

Hammersley, M. (1996) 'The relationship between qualitative and quantitative research: paradigm loyalty versus methodological eclecticism', in J.T.E. Richardson (ed.), *Handbook of Qualitative Research Methods for Psychology and the Social Sciences.* Leicester: BPS Books, pp. 159–74.

Hammersley, M. and Atkinson, P. (1983) *Ethnography: Principles in Practice.* London: Tavistock (2nd ed. 1995, Routledge).

Hesse-Biber, S. (2010a) 'Feminist approaches to mixed methods research: linking theory and praxis', in A. Tashakkori and C. Teddlie (eds), *The SAGE Handbook of Mixed Methods in Social and Behavioral Research*, 2nd ed. Thousand Oaks, CA: Sage, pp. 169–92.

Hesse-Biber, S. (2010b) 'Qualitative approaches to mixed methods practice', *Qualitative Inquiry*, 16 (6): 455–68.

Hesse-Biber, S.N. (2010c) *Mixed Methods Research: Merging Theory with Practice.* New York: Guilford.

Hesse-Biber, S. (2015) 'Mixed methods research: the "thing-ness" problem', *Qualitative Health Research*, 25 (6): 775–88.

Hesse-Biber, S. and Johnson, R.B. (eds) (2015) *The Oxford Handbook of Multimethod and Mixed Method Research Inquiry.* Oxford: Oxford University Press.

Hesse-Biber, S., Rodriguez, D. and Frost, N.A (2015) 'A qualitatively driven approach to multimethod and mixed methods research', in S. Hesse-Biber and R.B. Johnson (eds), *The Oxford Handbook of Multimethod and Mixed Method Research Inquiry.* Oxford: Oxford University Press, pp. 3–20.

Hildenbrand, B. (1999) *Fallrekonstruktive Familienforschung – Anleitungen für die Praxis.* Opladen: Leske & Budrich.

Hirschauer, S. and Amann, K. (eds) (1997) *Die Befremdung der eigenen Kultur. Zur ethnographischen Herausforderung soziologischer Empirie.* Frankfurt a. M.: Suhrkamp.

Hopf, C. (1982) 'Norm und Interpretation', *Zeitschrift für Soziologie*, 11: 309–27.

Hunter, A. and Brewer, J. (2006) *Foundations of Multimethod Research – Synthesizing Styles.* London: Sage.

Hunter, A. and Brewer, J. (2015) 'Designing multimethod research', in S. Hesse-Biber and R.B. Johnson (eds), *The Oxford Handbook of Multimethod and Mixed Method Research Inquiry.* Oxford: Oxford University Press, pp. 185–205.

Hurrelmann, K. and Albert, M. (eds) (2002) *Jugend 2002–14. Shell Jugendstudie.* Frankfurt a. M.: Fischer.

Jahoda, M. (1995) 'Jahoda, M., Lazarsfeld, P. and Zeisel, H.: Die Arbeitslosen von Marienthal', in U. Flick, E. von Kardorff, H. Keupp, L. von Rosenstiel and S. Wolff (eds), *Handbuch Qualitative Sozialforschung*, 2nd ed. Munich: Psychologie Verlags Union, pp. 119–22.

Jahoda, M., Lazarsfeld, P.F. and Zeisel, H. (1933/1971) *Marienthal: The Sociology of an Unemployed Community*. Chicago: Aldine-Atherton.

Jessor, R., Colby, A. and Shweder, R.A. (eds) (1996) *Ethnography and Human Development*. Chicago: Chicago University Press.

Jick, T. (1983) 'Mixing qualitative and quantitative methods: triangulation in action', in J. von Maanen (ed.), *Qualitative Methodology*. London: Sage, pp. 135–48.

Johnson, R.B. and Onwuegbuzie, A.J. (2004) 'Mixed methods research: a research paradigm whose time has come', *Educational Researcher*, 33 (7): 14–26.

Johnson, R.B. and Turner, L.S. (2003) 'Data collection strategies in mixed methods research', in A. Tashakkori and C. Teddlie (eds), *Handbook of Mixed Methods in Social and Behavioral Research*. Thousand Oaks, CA: Sage, pp. 297–319.

Johnson, R.B., Onwuegbuzie, A.J. and Turner, L.A. (2007) 'Towards a definition of mixed methods research: a research paradigm whose time has come', *Journal of Mixed Methods Research*, 1: 112–33.

Kelle, H. (2001) 'Ethnographische Methoden und Probleme der Triangulation – Am Beispiel der Peer Culture Forschung bei Kindern', *Zeitschrift für Soziologie der Erziehung und Sozialisation*, 21: 192–208.

Kelle, U. and Erzberger, C. (2004) 'Quantitative and qualitative methods: no confrontation', in U. Flick, E. von Kardorff and I. Steinke (eds), *A Companion to Qualitative Research*. London: Sage, pp. 172–7.

Kluge, S. (2001) 'Strategien zur Integration qualitativer und quantitativer Erhebungs- und Auswertungsverfahren. Ein methodischer und methodologischer Bericht aus dem Sonderforschungsbereich 186 "Statuspassagen und Risikolagen im Lebensverlauf"', in S. Kluge and U. Kelle (eds), *Methodeninnovation in der Lebenslaufforschung. Integration qualitativer und quantitativer Verfahren in der Lebenslauf- und Biographieforschung*. Weinheim: Juventa, pp. 37–88.

Knoblauch, H. (2004) 'The future prospects of qualitative research', in U. Flick, E. von Kardorff and I. Steinke (eds), *A Companion to Qualitative Research*. London: Sage, pp. 354–8.

Knoblauch, H., Flick, U. and Maeder, C. (eds) (2005) 'The state of the art of qualitative research in Europe', special issue of *Forum Qualitative Sozialforschung – FQS*, 6 (3). www. qualitative-research.net/index.php/fqs/issue/view/1.

Köckeis-Stangl, E. (1982) 'Methoden der Sozialisationsforschung', in K. Hurrelmann and D. Ulich (eds), *Handbuch der Sozialisationsforschung*. Weinheim: Beltz, pp. 321–70.

Kuckartz, U. (1995) 'Case-oriented quantification', in U. Kelle (ed.), *Computer-Aided Qualitative Data Analysis*. London: Sage, pp. 158–66.

Kuhn, T.S. (1962) *The Structure of Scientific Revolutions*. Chicago, IL: University of Chicago Press.

Lazarsfeld, P.F. (1960) 'Vorspruch zur neuen Auflage 1960', in M. Jahoda, P. Lazarsfeld and H. Zeisel, *Die Arbeitslosen von Marienthal*. Frankfurt a. M.: Suhrkamp, pp. 11–23.

Lincoln, Y.S. (2004) 'Norman Denzin', in U. Flick, E. von Kardorff and I. Steinke (eds), *A Companion to Qualitative Research*. London: Sage, pp. 53–7.

Lincoln, Y.S. and Guba, E.G. (1985) *Naturalistic Inquiry*. London: Sage.

Lüders, C. (1995) 'Von der Teilnehmenden Beobachtung zur ethnographischen Beschreibung – Ein Literaturbericht', in E. König and P. Zedler (eds), *Bilanz qualitativer Forschung*, Vol. 1. Weinheim: Deutscher Studienverlag, pp. 311–42.

Lüders, C. (2004a) 'Field observation and ethnography', in U. Flick, E. von Kardorff and I. Steinke (eds), *A Companion to Qualitative Research*. London: Sage, pp. 222–30.

Lüders, C. (2004b) 'The challenges of qualitative research', in U. Flick, E. von Kardorff and I. Steinke (eds), *A Companion to Qualitative Research*. London: Sage, pp. 359–64.

Lüders, C. and Reichertz, J. (1986) 'Wissenschaftliche Praxis ist, wenn alles funktioniert und keiner weiß warum: Bemerkungen zur Entwicklung qualitativer Sozialforschung', *Sozialwissenschaftliche Literaturrundschau*, 12: 90–102.

Lunt, P. and Livingstone, S. (1996) 'Rethinking the focus group in media and communications research', *Journal of Communication*, 46: 79–98.

Mallinson, S. (2002) 'Listening to respondents: a qualitative assessment of the Short-Form 36 Health Status Questionnaire', *Social Science and Medicine*, 54: 11–21.

Mark, M.M. and Shotland, R.L. (1987) 'Alternative models for the use of multiple methods', in M.M. Mark and R.L. Shotland (eds), *Multiple Methods in Program Evaluation: New Directions for Program Evaluation 35*. San Francisco: Jossey-Bass, pp. 95–100.

Marotzki, W. (1998) 'Ethnographische Verfahren in der Erziehungswissenschaftlichen Biographie Forschung', in G. Jüttemann and H. Thomae (eds), *Biographische Methoden in den Humanwissenschaften*. Weinheim: Beltz, pp. 44–59.

Mathison, S. (1988) 'Why triangulate?', *Educational Researcher*, 17 (2): 13–17.

Maxwell, J.A. (1992) 'Understanding and validity in qualitative research', *Harvard Educational Review*, 62: 279–300.

Maxwell, J.A. (2016) 'Expanding the history and range of mixed methods research', *Journal of Mixed Methods Research*, 10: 12–27.

Miles, M.B. and Huberman, A.M. (1984) *Qualitative Data Analysis: An Expanded Sourcebook*. Thousand Oaks, CA: Sage.

Miles, M.B. and Huberman, A.M. (1994) *Qualitative Data Analysis: A Sourcebook of New Methods*, 2nd ed. Newbury Park, CA: Sage.

Mishler, E.G. (1986) 'The analysis of interview-narratives', in T.R. Sarbin (ed.), *Narrative Psychology*. New York: Praeger, pp. 233–55.

Morgan, D.L. (1988) *Focus Groups as Qualitative Research*. Newbury Park, CA: Sage.

Morgan, D. (1998) 'Practical strategies for combining qualitative and quantitative methods: application to health research', *Qualitative Health Research*, 8: 362–76.

Morgan, D.L. (2007) 'Paradigms lost and pragmatism regained: methodological implications of combining qualitative and quantitative methods', *Journal of Mixed Methods Research*, 1: 48–76.

Morgan, D.L. (2014) *Integrating Qualitative and Quantitative Methods: A Pragmatic Approach.* Thousand Oaks, CA: Sage.

Morris, J., Murphy, K., Nonemaker, S., Hawes, C., Phillips, C., Fries, B. and Mor, V. (1995) *Long Term Care Resident Assessment Instrument. Users Manual 2.0.* Chapel Hill, NC: Research Triangle Institute.

Morse, J.M. (1998) 'Designing funded qualitative research', in N. Denzin and Y.S. Lincoln (eds), *Strategies of Qualitative Research.* London: Sage, pp.56–85.

Morse, J.M. (2003) 'Principles of mixed methods and multimethod designs', in A. Tashakkori and C. Teddlie (eds), *Handbook of Mixed Methods in Social and Behavioral Research.* Thousand Oaks, CA: Sage, pp. 189–208.

Morse, J.M. (2010) 'Simultaneous and sequential qualitative mixed method designs', *Qualitative Inquiry*, 16 (6): 483–91.

Morse, J. (2014) 'Making room for qualitatively-driven mixed-method research', *Qualitative Health Research*, 24 (1): 3–5.

Morse, J.M. and Maddox, L. (2014) 'Analytic strategies with qualitative components in mixed-method research', in U. Flick (ed.) *The SAGE Handbook of Qualitative Data Analysis.* London: Sage, pp. 524–39.

Morse, J., Swanson, J.M. and Kunzel, A.J. (eds) (2001) *The Nature of Qualitative Evidence.* Thousand Oaks, CA: Sage.

Moscovici, S. (1998) 'The history and actuality of social representations', in U. Flick (ed.), *The Psychology of the Social.* Cambridge: Cambridge University Press, pp. 209–47.

Neisser, U. (1981) 'John Dean's memory: a case study', *Cognition*, 9 (1):1–22.

O'Cathain, A. (2010) 'Assessing the quality of mixed methods research', in A. Tashakkori and C. Teddlie (eds), *The SAGE Handbook of Mixed Methods in Social and Behavioral Research*, 2nd ed. Thousand Oaks, CA: Sage, pp. 531–57.

O'Cathain, A., Murphy, E. and Nicholl, J. (2008) 'The quality of mixed methods studies in health services research', *Journal of Health Services Research & Policy*, 13 (2): 92–8.

Patton, M.Q. (1980) *Qualitative Evaluation Methods.* Beverly Hills, CA: Sage.

Patton, M.Q. (2015) *Qualitative Evaluation and Research Methods*, 4th ed. London: Sage.

Picot, S. and Willert, M. (2002) 'Politik per Klick – Internet und Engagement Jugendlicher', in Deutsche Shell (ed.) *Jugend 2002. Zwischen pragmatischem Idealismus und robustem Materialismus, 14. Shell Jugendstudie*, Frankfurt: Fischer, pp. 221–414.

Plano Clark, V. and Badiee, M. (2010) 'Research questions in mixed methods research', in A. Tashakkori and C. Teddlie (eds), *The SAGE Handbook of Mixed Methods in Social and Behavioral Research*, 2nd ed. Thousand Oaks, CA: Sage, pp. 275–304.

Polanyi, M. (1966) *The Tacit Dimension.* New York: Doubleday.

Polkinghorne, D. (1988) *Narrative Knowing and the Human Sciences.* Albany: State University of New York.

Preissle, J., Glover-Kudon, R.M., Rohan, E.A., Boehm, J.E. and DeGroff, A. (2015) 'Putting ethics on the mixed methods map', in S.N. Hesse-Biber and R.B. Johnson (eds), *The Oxford Handbook of Multimethod and Mixed Methods Research Inquiry.* Oxford: Oxford University Press, pp. 144–63.

Rapley, T. (2018) *Doing Conversation, Discourse and Document Analysis* (Book 7 of *The SAGE Qualitative Research Kit*, 2nd ed.). London: Sage.

Reichertz, J. (2004) 'Objective hermeneutics and hermeneutic sociology of knowledge,', in U. Flick, E.v. Kardorff, and I. Steinke (eds.), *A Companion to Qualitative Research*. London: Sage, pp. 290–5.

Richardson, L. (2000) 'Writing: a method of inquiry', in N. Denzin and Y.S. Lincoln (eds.), *Handbook of Qualitative Research*, 2nd ed. London: Sage, pp. 923–48.

Robinson, J.A. and Hawpe, L. (1986) 'Narrative thinking as a heuristic process', in T.R. Sarbin (ed.), *Narrative Psychology: The Storied Nature of Human Conduct*. New York: Praeger, pp. 111–84.

Rock, P. (2001) 'Symbolic interactionism and ethnography', in P. Atkinson, A. Coffey, S. Delamont, J. Lofland and L. Lofland (eds), *Handbook of Ethnography*. London: Sage, pp. 26–39.

Roller, E., Mathes, R. and Eckert, T. (1995) 'Hermeneutic-classificatory content analysis', in U. Kelle (ed.), *Computer-Aided Qualitative Data Analysis*. London: Sage, pp. 167–76.

Sandelowski, M. (2003) 'Tables or tableaux? The challenges of writing and reading mixed methods studies', in A. Tashakkori and C. Teddlie (eds), *Handbook of Mixed Methods in Social and Behavioral Research*. Thousand Oaks, CA: Sage, pp. 321–50.

Sandelowski, M. (2014) 'Unmixing mixed-methods research', *Research in Nursing & Health*, 37: 3–8.

Saukko, P. (2003) *Doing Research in Cultural Studies*. London: Sage.

Schönberger, C. and von Kardorff, E. (2004) *Mit dem kranken Partner leben*. Opladen: Leske & Budrich.

Schütze, F. (1994) 'Ethnographie und sozialwissenschaftliche Methoden der Feldforschung', in N. Groddeck and M. Schmann (eds), *Modernisierung Sozialer Arbeit durch Methodenentwicklung und – reflexion*. Freiburg: Lambertus, pp. 189–288.

Silverman, D. (1985) *Qualitative Methodology and Sociology*. Aldershot: Gower.

Smith, H.W. (1975) *Strategies for Social Research*. Englewood Cliffs, NJ: Prentice-Hall.

Sparkes, A. (2001) 'Myth 94: qualitative researchers will agree about validity', *Qualitative Health Research*, 11 (4): 538–52.

Spradley, J.P. (1979) *The Ethnographic Interview*. New York: Holt, Rinehart & Winston.

Spradley, J.P. (1980) *Participant Observation*. New York: Holt, Rinehart & Winston.

Strauss, A.L. (1987) *Qualitative Analysis for Social Scientists*. Cambridge: Cambridge University Press.

Strauss, A.L., Schatzman, L., Bucher, R., Ehrlich, D. and Sabshin, M. (1964) *Psychiatric Ideologies and Institutions*. New York: Free Press of Glencoe.

Strube, G. (1989) *Episodisches Wissen*. Arbeitspapiere der GMD (385), pp. 10–26.

Symonds, J. and Gorard, S. (2010) 'Death of mixed methods? Or the rebirth of research as a craft', *Evaluation & Research in Education*, 23: 121–36.

Tashakkori, A. and Teddlie, C. (eds) (2003a) *Handbook of Mixed Methods in Social and Behavioral Research*. Thousand Oaks, CA: Sage.

Tashakkori, A. and Teddlie, C. (2003b) 'Major issues and controversies in the use of mixed methods in social and behavioral research', in A. Tashakkori and C. Teddlie (eds), *Handbook of Mixed Methods in Social and Behavioral Research*. Thousand Oaks, CA: Sage, pp. 3–50.

Tashakkori, A. and Teddlie, C. (2003c) 'The past and future of mixed methods research: from data triangulation to mixed model designs', in A. Tashakkori and C. Teddlie (eds), *Handbook of Mixed Methods in Social and Behavioral Research*. Thousand Oaks, CA: Sage, pp. 671–700.

Tashakkori, A. and Teddlie, C. (eds) (2010) *The SAGE Handbook of Mixed Methods in Social and Behavioral Research*, 2nd ed. Thousand Oaks, CA: Sage.

Teddlie, C. and Tashakkori, A. (2009) *Foundations of Mixed Methods Research: Integrating Quantitative and Qualitative Approaches in the Social and Behavioral Sciences*. London: Sage.

Thomas, W.I. and Znaniecki, F. (1918–20) *The Polish Peasant in Europe and America*, Vols 1–2. New York: Knopf.

Tracy, S.J. (2010) 'Qualitative quality: eight "big-tent" criteria for excellent qualitative research', *Qualitative Inquiry*, 16: 837–51.

Tulving, E. (1972) 'Episodic and semantic memory', in E. Tulving and W. Donaldson (eds), *Organization of Memory*. New York: Academic Press, pp. 381–403.

Walter, U., Flick, U., Fischer, C., Neuber, A. and Schwartz, F.-W. (2006) *Alter und Gesundheit. Subjektive Vorstellungen von Ärzten und Pflegekräften*. Opladen: VS-Verlag für Sozialwissenschaften.

Webb, E.J., Campbell, D.T., Schwartz, R.D. and Sechrest, L. (1966) *Unobtrusive Measures: Nonreactive Research in the Social Sciences*. Chicago: Rand McNally.

Wertz, F.J., Charmaz, K., McMullen, L.M., Josselson, R., Anderson, R. and McSpadden, E. (2011) *Five Ways of Doing Qualitative Analysis*. New York: Guilford.

Westie, F.R. (1957) 'Towards closer relations between theory and research: a procedure and an example', *American Sociological Review*, 22: 149–54.

Whyte, W.F. (1955) *Street Corner Society*, enlarged ed. Chicago: University of Chicago Press.

Wilson, T. (1981) 'Qualitative "versus" quantitative research', in M. Küchler, T.P. Wilson and D.H. Zimmerman (eds), *Integration von qualitativen und quantitativen Forschungsansätzen*. Mannheim: ZUMA, pp. 37–69.

Wolff, S. (2004) 'Ways into the field and their variants', in U. Flick, E. von Kardorff and I. Steinke (eds), *A Companion to Qualitative Research*. London: Sage, pp. 195–202.

INDEX